THE GERALD KRAAK ANTHOLOGY:
AFRICAN PERSPECTIVES ON GENDER,
SOCIAL JUSTICE AND SEXUALITY

As You Like It

First published by Jacana Media (Pty) Ltd, in partnership with
The Other Foundation, in 2018

10 Orange Street
Sunnyside
Auckland Park 2092
South Africa
+2711 628 3200
www.jacana.co.za

ISBN 978-1-4314-2666-9

Cover design by Shawn Paikin
Set in Stempel Garamond 10.5/16pt
Job no. 003246

solutions
Printed by **novus print**, a Novus Holdings company

See a complete list of Jacana titles at www.jacana.co.za

Contents

Foreword

Africa's 'newest genre': The queer Afro-modern

Afro-moderns are … homosexuals, heterosexuals, bisexuals, transexuals and whateversexuals burning to rescue this continent from the ruins of stupid black men. We are not only the turning-point generation; we are also Africa's hugest turning, biggest point and boldest generation…

   We are neither a theory nor a movement. We are open space: Africa's newest genre.

With these words from his winning essay, the Nigerian writer Pwaangulongii Dauod lays down the challenge to this year's Gerald Kraak Prize, and the anthology that has come out of it. Such a project promises the thrill but also the danger of 'open space', of uncharted territories and exploded taboos. And here is both the pathos and the call to arms of this year's competition: the writer of the above words, our very winner, must use a pseudónym, as he has already been subject to an attack that forced him to flee his hometown after his essay, 'Africa's future has no space for stupid black men', was first published in 2016.

Another shortlisted contributor from Nigeria, Hapuya Ononime, must also remain anonymous. After he was outed as gay in a country with the harshest anti-homosexuality laws on the planet – outside of Muslim Sharia – he was kidnapped, beaten and held ransom. His poem cycle, 'Reclamation', is a meditation on this experience of having been so violently othered. Sarah Lubala's poems, set in central and southern Africa, and Tshepiso Mabula's photographic essay, of an eviction in downtown Johannesburg, deal with different issues: forced migrancy and gender. But they have this in common with the Nigerian writers, and indeed with all the shortlisted works: they provide what we might call a "queer" perspective, that of the outsider.

In some instances, they do so in bracing manifesto form, such as in Chibụihè Obi's 'We are queer, we are here' or Nick Hadikwa Mwaluko's 'XXYX Africa: More invisible'. In others, they use reportage to offer the sense of a transgender woman's life in Johannesburg (Carl Collison's 'Princess') or the phenomenon of Ugandan LGBT refugees in Kenya (Isaac Otidi's 'Facing the Mediterranean').

Many use fiction and reportage to unpeel the double lives that queer Africans endure, as in Chiké Frankie Edozien's 'The Shea prince', David Medalie's 'Borrowed by the wind', Jayne Bauling's 'Full moon', Welcome Lishivha's 'Site visits' and Kiprop Kimutai's 'The man at the bridge'. What is so rich about these narratives is the way their protagonists – or subjects, or authors – find strength and creativity in the "queerness" that results from such a bifurcated existence.

This creativity is manifest not only in the content of this collection, but in its form too. Tiffany Mugo and Siphomeze Khundayi compose a collage of testimony and image to advance an African lesbian BDSM aesthetic; Thandokuhle Mngqibisa works with verse and auto-portraiture to explore gender in society. Pierre de Vos and Jaco Barnard-Naude, like Efemia Chela, bust genres to meld criticism and theory with memoir – and humour.

Chibu̧ihè Obi concludes his essay with the following lines: 'We have refused invisibility ... We are here ... Finally we are here.' All these writers and artists celebrate this fact, but they do not shy away from the hard realities that come with such visibility. This generation of Afro-Moderns are staking new territory, by bringing to the surface identities and practices long submerged. The state-sanctioned homophobia described in this collection in countries like Nigeria and Uganda is a backlash against the Afro-Moderns, determined to live their lives according to notions of personal autonomy that are anathema to the patriarchy Dauod derides.

But even those works set in 'enlightened' South Africa express the doubleness that comes with being queer: that gap between being protected by the constitution and the reality of the strictures of life on the street, or the village, or even just in a family. If creativity is one hallmark of the Afro-Modern, then resilience is another.

Ephemia Chela is the daughter of evangelical Christians who will not affirm her sexuality. At the end of her review of Maggie Nelson's pathbreaking memoir, The Argonauts, Chela writes that the book authorises her own quest 'for a more flexible world'. She describes The Argonauts as a book about 'living and loving in-between: in between life and death, male and female, law and lawlessness, love and indifference, language and ideas'.

We, the judges of this, the 2018 Gerald Kraak Award, have similar aspirations for the book you hold in your hands. This year, the judges were Sisonke Msimang – our chair – along with Sylvia Tamale and myself. We received 482 entries from fourteen countries, although the bulk were from South Africa and Nigeria. We deeply hope to get a more diverse spread in the years to come, as Gerald Kraak becomes a new benchmark for the Afro-Modern; for the "open space" that is being staked, at the confluence of literary creativity and human rights advocacy, specifically around gender and sexuality.

The Gerald Kraak Award is a joint initiative of the The Other Foundation and the Jacana Literary Foundation. This book would not have been possible without the vision and dedication of Neville

Gabriel and Samuel Shapiro at the former, and Sibongile Machika and Andisiwe Madavha at the latter. Sisonke Msimang has brought passion and intellect to leading the process, and in editing this book. Her introduction, which follows, is literature itself: a gorgeous praise-poem for the Afro-modern.

– Mark Gevisser

Editor's note
Crossings

THIS YEAR THE ANTHOLOGY HAS grown considerably – almost doubling in size. These stories take up space; they are big and heavy and weighty and solid. These stories make no apologies. The sentences you will find on these pages are not afraid. They move from the brutal and the bloody to the melodic and the lyrical. They are crisp and controlled then suddenly they melt; sweetly, seductively. There is romance and laughter and the bittersweet markings of missed opportunities and hard-won battles. The pages of this book are adorned with paragraphs that run on and on, and with poems that beg to continue. They shimmer with idiom and sparkle with words whose beauty lies in their refusal to be translated from pidgin and Igbo and Kalenjin. This collection is queer and it is coal and dust and it is diamonds and so it is African.

The words you will read in this collection spill out in bewildering certainty, running across the pages as though they have no end. There are short stories that could be books and essays whose word-counts we had to limit only because of the practicalities of printing an object that must find its way into shops and then into hands and then onto shelves in homes where it will be loved and read and pored over and read again and fought over and made love to as though it weren't words at all, but songs on a favourite album. The poems in this collection are a mixtape – written to be read and also to be spoken aloud by friends and lovers. The photos are portraits of people and communities that are often under pressure but refuse to be fractured. They too are a song.

This year, in this collection you will find stories whose characters could talk forever, whose plotlines twist and turn, whose subtlety makes you draw in your breath.

The stories in this collection take up space and they are not sorry.

The judges this year selected work that we liked: work that was funny and evocative and sometimes just simple and pretty but always political. We did not have an overarching theme or focus. But when writing is grounded in politics, themes cannot help themselves: they burst and they bubble and they boil over, speaking to one another across poems and calling out to one another over essays and bumping into each other in phrases parsed in different ways but similar nonetheless in photos that mirror one another.

And so, even with their weight and their determination to be big and to take up space, each of the stories in this collection is, at heart, about the ways in which queer people cross borders and enter territories. They are about the ways in which queers are travellers and women who don't fit the mould are transgressors. The collection reminds us that survival requires an imperative to move or die. Indeed, many of the stories we selected are about the compulsion to die – the choice to cross into the realm of death rather than live through disrespect and derision and denial. On a continent where your gayness or your femininity or your refusal to conform to gender norms will get you chased from home or run out of town, the crossings catalogued in this book are not simply metaphorical – they are devastatingly real.

So we have gathered together stories of queer people who are moving, crossing, travelling, always journeying. The collection contains submissions by some of the finest and freshest writers the continent has to offer. There are also pieces in this collection by activists who are deeply invested in ideas that will change conversations about women and men and homosexuality and culture. The photo essays have been produced by women and queer people who look at their communities with grace and wit and compassion. Above all, this book flaunts the abundance of intellectual riches this continent has to offer.

Finally, it would be foolish to end this introduction without providing a taste of what lies inside. This year, in addition to the overall winner of the prize – 'Africa's future has no place for stupid black men' by Pwaangulongii Dauod, we have recognised three highly commended selections in the categories of Photography, Fiction and Poetry. Kiprop Kimutai and Sarah Lubala respectively, are recognised as highly commended selections in their fields.

Each of these pieces, in their own way, embodies the journeys and crossings that tie this collection together.

In the angry, mournful and confrontingly triumphant 'Africa's future has no place for stupid black men', Dauod paints a picture of a community that refuses to be dependent on external ideas of itself. Crossing that line – to self definition – is a source of tremendous pride even as it signals a death warrant. Those who dare to insist that

> 'We are neither a theory nor a movement. We are open space: Africa's newest genre. We are the unemployables, dissidents, techies, pan-Africanists, designers, etc. coming out in the 21st century, in our different corners, to challenge the centuries-old notion that Africa does little thinking, trades badly, and is even worse at buying ... Afro-Moderns know how badly their stupid forefathers performed in the past and are now refusing to mourn it.'

In Kiprop Kimutai's 'The man at the bridge' (highly commended fiction selection), the opening paragraph is nothing if not transporting.

Just after Riaku Bridge, a place where trees congregated at night, Kwambai saw the glint in a man's eyes and stopped his car. Stepping out, he peered into the dark. It was late so most men had gone, leaving behind only the most determined. The man was leaning on the rails of the bridge, his hands tucked in his tight jeans as if he possessed the night.

From Kimutai's 'Bridge', we move to Sarah Lubala's poem (highly commended poetry selection), 'Portraits of a border girl'. Lubala's words have a haunting lyricism, asking questions that demand answers and yet to which there can never be responses:

Tell me
where do I put her?
this girl pressed against the border
this girl swallowing her papers whole
this girl bird-wailing through a fence

In the pages of this anthology – as in life – journeying is often a capitulation or a choice that is no choice at all – merely a last, exhausted resort. Yet time and again the sojourners who populate these pages are engaged in the work of hope. Often, journeying is in fact a decision, a choiceless choice, a sacred attempt to find freedom and community on the other side of a bridge, a fence and, yes, even of morality.

– Sisonke Msimang

Facing the Mediterranean[1]

ISAAC OTIDI AMUKE

FOR THE LAST FIVE DECADES, KENYA and Uganda have had an unofficial pact of providing a passageway for each other's escapees. This started with the 1971 Idi Amin overthrow of Milton Obote, which saw a mass exodus of Ugandans into Kenya and elsewhere in the world. The other mass exodus happened in 1986. The second Milton Obote government was overthrown by Brigadier Bazilio Olara-Okello and General Tito Okello. Following the post-coup chaos, the Yoweri Museveni-led National Resistance Army (NRA) seized power. Some say that back then all it took for a Langi or an Acholi – the two ethnic communities perceived to be Obote's main supporters – to be granted asylum in the United Kingdom was money for an air ticket to London. Kenyan opposition figures have also always snuck into Uganda when things

---

1 Previously published by Commonwealth Writers on 27 July 2015, http://www.commonwealthwriters.org/facing-the-mediterranean/

got heated, an example being Raila Odinga, who fled to Norway through Uganda.

Today the story is different.

There is no military takeover in Uganda, and Kampala has not fallen. Yet there are growing numbers of Ugandan refugees and asylum seekers in Kenya. These particular Ugandans, mainly in their 20s, say they are running away from home because of their sexuality and whom they choose to love.

It all began in early 2011, when a group of Ugandans on a journey to an unknown destination was intercepted by Kenyan police in the Northern Kenya town of Lodwar. On interrogation, the group told the police they were Ugandan lesbian, gay, bisexual, transgender and intersex asylum seekers escaping persecution back home. They were on their way to seek refuge at the Kakuma refugee camp, not too far away from Lodwar. At this point, the police didn't know what to do with them.

They made a phone call.

'Ray,[2] come and see your people.'

Ray quickly understood what the policeman meant by 'his people'.

Ray worked for an organisation that supports LGBTI refugees and asylum seekers both in Lodwar and at Kakuma. He was used to dealing with Kenyans, but he had never interacted with Ugandan asylum seekers before. This was the first group of LGBTI Ugandans arriving in Kakuma. Today, four years later, over 200 Ugandan asylum seekers have gone through Kakuma, hopeful they too will get lucky and be resettled.

Having got a sense of things from my Nairobi base, I was curious to understand how these young LGBTI Ugandans found themselves having to run to the border and out of their country. I wanted to look at what had changed both in Uganda in general and inside the bureaucracies responsible for their safe passage in the years since then. I spent just under a fortnight shuttling between Kampala and Nairobi having hour-long conversations at different times with a

---

2   The names of individuals have been changed to protect their privacy.

2

minimum of ten individuals – including refugees and asylum seekers in Nairobi, resettled refugees in Europe and America, leaders of the LGBTI movement on both sides of the border, UNHCR officials and representatives from their partner organisations, human rights lawyers and academics. In the end, there were no easy answers to the questions I raised, a realisation that almost everyone I spoke to agreed with.

LIKE THE WEATHER (PART 1)

Conversations in Kampala
Outside the nightclub a group of men dressed for a fashion show are holding court – one of them dressed in screaming pink tights is strutting up and down the driveway. Inside the club, an elderly gentleman is seated at the main counter. Middle-aged lovers on long stools lean over to reach their partners. Younger revellers are the more restless lot, manoeuvring the dance floor looking stylish and leaving a lingering trail of perfumes and colognes. In this scene, as the song says, 'age ain't nothing but a number.'

The week I am in Kampala everyone has told me I have to check out this particular place on Sunday night. They tell me it's where I'll see what they've been saying about living as lesbian, gay, bisexual, transgender or intersex people in Uganda. The point about this nightclub is that every Sunday night, LGBTI Ugandans gather here and have a party like no other. And this is precisely what they have been saying: 'While Ugandan society – as in many other African countries – discriminates against gay people, life here isn't awful. In fact, there's even a gay scene.' Tonight Sandra Ntebi takes me to the party. Sandra is the chairperson of the Lesbian, Gay, Bisexual, Transgender and Intersex National Security Committee, an umbrella body that deals with security concerns of LGBTI Ugandans across the country, whether they're affiliated to any organisation or not. Sandra tells me the reason he's agreed to come with me is because he wants to show me a side of Uganda people rarely talk about, the side where lesbian, gay, bisexual, transgender and intersex

Ugandans from across the social spectrum have a good time without looking over their shoulders to see who's watching.

Once inside the nightclub, Sandra walks me around. We see young men and women making out with their same-sex partners and giving each other lap dances. Sandra keeps asking me whether what I am seeing is in line with the narrative that LGBTI Ugandans are all hiding because the country is impossible to live in.

'Can you believe this is the same Uganda people keep talking about?'

Sandra and I happen on an altercation between two gentlemen. One of them is challenging the other – seemingly his partner:

'Why did you go to Kenya? Why? Why did you go to Kenya? Was it for the excitement?'

During my stay in Uganda I quickly learn that the word on the street is – and has been for some time now – that a good story about persecution based on one's sexuality can translate into passage to Europe or America. I am told this situation once led to a bus full of Ugandans arriving in Nairobi, all of its passengers claiming to be LGBTI asylum seekers.

As Sandra and I stand with our drinks in Kampala, over 200 Ugandans are already registered by both the United Nations High Commissioner for Refugees and the Kenyan government's Department of Refugee Affairs (DRA) as refugees and asylum seekers on grounds of persecution for their sexual orientation. Most of these applicants can count on UNHCR resettlement to third countries. Now both the UNHCR and its implementing partner organisations have raised a red flag that there is a real possibility the asylum process is being abused by some Ugandans, given the unexpected numbers crossing the border into Kenya.

According to official UNHCR documents,[3] the present crisis began

---

3 In January 2015 the UNHCR sent out to its NGO partner organisations a document titled 'The Updated UNHCR 5 Key Messages 2015' detailing its five-point positions on key issues affecting LGBTI refugees and asylum seekers in Kenya, with a particular focus on the Ugandans and how the organisation had decided to handle their caseload.

in 2014 when a handful of Ugandan escapees showed up at UNHCR in Nairobi and at Kakuma refugee camp in Northern Kenya. They were all seeking asylum, citing the passage of the Anti-Homosexuality Act[4] in Uganda as one of their reasons for fearing for their safety. Seeing that they were dealing with a small and manageable group and knowing the high risk they faced in a foreign country where homosexuality is also criminalised, the UNHCR sped up the group's caseload, giving them priority across all its processes. This included the provision of financial support – which was in addition to the psychosocial support given to all refugees. The UNHCR worked hard to facilitate speedy resettlement in third countries for this particular group of Ugandans, further securing their safety.

The mistake UNHCR made, it would appear, was to imagine that this was an isolated group of Ugandans and that there wouldn't be more coming. These initial actions, noble as they were, came back to haunt the UNHCR and its partners.

Before long, word got back to Kampala that there was a direct passage either to Europe or America if one pitched up at the UNHCR in Nairobi or Kakuma citing persecution based on sexuality. It was said that there would even be financial assistance as one awaited resettlement. This is how, from late 2014, the UNHCR started paying the price for its earlier expediency.

Now Ugandans would arrive every other week citing persecution on account of their sexuality. Over time it was not unheard of for someone to cross the border into Kenya, register as a refugee or an asylum seeker before sneaking back into Uganda. Then one could return to Nairobi every month to pick up the monthly UNHCR stipend but continue to live in Uganda while awaiting resettlement.

---

4   The Uganda Anti Homosexuality Act – which criminalised same-sex relations and proposed life imprisonment and penalties for individuals, companies, media/other organisations supporting homosexual people – was passed in December 2013 by the Ugandan parliament. The Act was struck down by the Constitutional Court of Uganda in August 2014.

With these developments the UNHCR decided to pull the plug on prioritising the Ugandan LGBTI caseload. There would be no further financial assistance and the caseload would follow normal UNHCR procedure without exemptions. The effect of this, of course, was that that genuine LGBTI refugees and asylum seekers could no longer have the much-needed protection. Unless one had an urgent medical emergency or similar life-threatening condition the UNHCR was no longer making exceptions for anyone related to any matter at all.

Yet, the reality is, of course, homophobia is alive and well both in Uganda and in refugee camps, and that the clampdown has had some unintended – though certainly easily anticipated – consequences.

By way of example, it is worth examining a confidential email I was able to examine. Dated March 2015, it was sent by a staffer of a Christian charity working at the Kakuma refugee camp and addressed to a senior UNHCR official in Nairobi, with a number of other officials copied. The message addressed the issue of three (LGBTI?) asylum seekers. They had arrived at a refugee camp in Northern Kenya in early March. Since their arrival they had been sleeping on the floor at the UNHCR reception centre, which is where all new arrivals at the camp stay until the UNHCR processes their information and admits them to the camp. The email noted that the three individuals had not been given any food. When the author of the email asked a UNHCR official about this, the official said he was not responsible for the situation. To make matters worse, when the three went out in search of food from the South Sudanese community within the camp – which is one of the largest communities within Kakuma – they got back and found all their belongings missing.

Seeing no improvement in their condition, they decided to walk to Nairobi, but were intercepted by UNHCR and following the intervention of an organisation named in the email just by its initials, URM, they were taken back to a holding place near the camp.

The author of the email signed off by appealing to its recipients for action: the three Ugandans had still not been registered by UNHCR and lacked what she called the ability for 'basic survival', in that they were still not receiving food because they had not been registered. The final plea in the email was on the basis that the three had also run out of cash, after using whatever last coin they had to buy food.

The email indicated that the Ugandans had lost their special status, whether one blames opportunists feigning persecution, a lack of urgency by the UNHCR or the inadequacy of funds and facilities to sustain an ever-increasing number of refugees and asylum seekers. Whatever the cause, these are now the circumstances faced by LGBTI Ugandans escaping persecution. Their suffering was apparently increased by the distrust the UNHCR developed for the number of Ugandans streaming in, and there is belief among these refugees that even if one's case merits prioritising it might take longer than expected for it to be processed. The Ugandans are hoping the UNHCR will reverse its hard stance, while the UNHCR is hoping the Ugandans will adjust their expectations according to UNHCR procedures. It seems they are both waiting to see who will blink first.

When I met Sandra for the first time and had a lengthy conversation about the state of the LGBTI movement in Uganda and the level of risk faced by the average gay person in the country, he took a surprisingly categorical stance. It wasn't one I expected. I live in Kenya and I had been aware that a number of organisations in Nairobi, including the UNHCR, had registered a dramatic escalation in the number of Ugandans arriving in Kenya claiming persecution because of their sexuality. I had a strong impression that Uganda was completely unsafe for LGBTI people.

'Uganda is not the worst place to live as a gay person,' Sandra said.

Sandra made the point that those living openly as members of the Ugandan LGBTI movement can often do so because they have a relative amount of privilege. They are more physically secure because of the neighbourhoods where they live, the jobs they hold, the families they come from, the friendships and social networks they maintain, the places they choose to hang out, and so on.

'We have genuine cases needing assistance but everyone cannot now say being gay in Uganda is an automatic death sentence. I am a proud Ugandan. I love my country. I vote. I pay tax. I live like any other

Ugandan. We have our challenges as a country. But Uganda is not the worst place to live in whether one is gay or not,' Sandra said. A few days later, I sought out Richard Lusimbo, research and documentation manager at Sexual Minorities Uganda (SMUG), Uganda's umbrella LGBTI organisation. I told him about my Sunday night escapades, asking him to enlighten me as to how gay Ugandans regularly have a night out at a known location, without anyone showing up and throwing them into police trucks.

Richard told me the Ugandan LGBTI movement had progressively built political capital and, as such, concessions have been made in some places for things like Sunday night to happen. The concessions are made in backrooms, he said, because at the end of the day gay Ugandans are Ugandan citizens who can be given a hearing in any office. Not that things are always smooth. He was just back from Mbarara in Western Uganda where a group of nine men had been arrested on suspicion of being gay. They had been paraded and ridiculed, and while in police custody had been forcibly subjected to HIV/AIDS testing and compulsory anal testing – supposedly to confirm whether they were gay.

This is how fluid things are in Uganda. The ground can shift fast from the Sunday night party to the Tuesday morning report of violations.

Richard told me it was unfortunate that hoards of Ugandans were fleeing into Kenya and having to put up with deplorable conditions. He and his colleague and fellow firefighter Douglas Mawidra, SMUG's human rights officer, strongly believe no Ugandan should have to flee their home because of their sexuality. Lusimbo pointed out that SMUG (as the umbrella LGBTI organisation) has never suggested that anyone should leave the country; it prioritises home-grown solutions, fighting homophobia and building systems to make LGBTI Ugandans secure.

Both Lusimbo and Mawidra told me those who choose to flee do so on their own volition without the prompting of any organisation, since asylum-seeking is a legal process that may be pursued by any individual who believes they're facing persecution. SMUG has, however, responded to the growing exodus by developing an emergency response service that allows it to answer distress calls from anywhere in the country within 24 hours. This is in part a response to the impression created, amid growing claims of persecution and evidence of migration, that there are no comprehensive local interventions in Uganda to assist those in need.

* * *

I am trying to resolve the conflict in my mind, comparing the Sunday night party with Tuesday morning's reports of harassment in Mbarara, and find myself standing between two compelling realities. On the one hand, here are individuals who can party at the nightclub in Kampala and, on the other hand, there are men persecuted for the mere suggestion that they might be gay. I put my dilemma to Lusimbo. He responded by quoting Dr Frank Mugisha, SMUG's executive director – who was out of the country when I visited: 'Uganda is like the weather. Today can be sunny. Tomorrow can be rainy. You can never tell.'

I decided I needed more answers.

CAN'T GO BACK (PART 2)

Talking to two Ugandan refugees

For Wilberforce[5] – a gay Ugandan refugee – resettlement couldn't have come sooner.

Wilberforce's partner had come visiting at his apartment, like he always did. Once the two were settled inside they heard a knock on the door and opened it to find his partner's brother, who worked for the Ugandan military. Like the rest of their families, the brother didn't approve of their same-sex relationship. He had tracked them down to Wilberforce's place, where he believed the two spent time nurturing their secret relationship.

---

5   The names of individuals have been changed to protect their privacy.

On entering the house, he pounced on Wilberforce and started beating him up. When his partner tried to intervene, he received a beating of his own – worse than what had been meted out to Wilberforce. His head was crushed hard against the concrete floor. By the time the situation was contained and the brother restrained by Wilberforce, it was already too late. Wilberforce's partner had suffered internal head injuries that resulted in a fatal brain haemorrhage. Wilberforce almost breaks down narrating this to me on the phone.

Wilberforce's father disowned him after the incident, telling him he was no longer his son and asking him never to be in touch with his family. His father's decree came after the publication of names of gay Ugandans by a leading tabloid. He had escaped the tabloid's net, but people around him had started suspecting that he and his lover were having a relationship. Once his lover's brother struck, there was nowhere for Wilberforce to hide.

He abandoned his comfortable life in Kampala and fled to Nairobi.

Once in Nairobi, Wilberforce contacted UNHCR, which advised him to find his way to Kakuma refugee camp. He took a bus from Nairobi to Eldoret, a town in the Kenyan Rift Valley. From there he took a second bus to Kitale and it was already 2 am when he started the next journey to Lodwar in arid Northern Kenya, before the final four-hour journey to Kakuma. Here he met other Ugandans on the run from persecution. This made Wilberforce part of the early group of Ugandans who arrived in Kenya in 2011 and whose caseload was prioritised and fast-tracked by the UNHCR.

The Makerere University graduate lived for two-and-a-half years in the Kakuma refugee camp in the semi desert of Northern Kenya. When life got unbearable – as he says it does for everyone at the camp and especially for gay and transgender refugees and asylum seekers – Wilberforce would contemplate leaving to come and live in Nairobi. But he opted to stay on, since in Nairobi he would be on his own with no direct support from UNHCR. Kakuma was hell, he says, but at least UNHCR was present, providing tents, basic healthcare and food.

Wilberforce says they were very few Ugandans in those early days, all of them living in an enclosed area which made them lonely and vulnerable to other groups in the camp. Yet Wilberforce is in fact most sympathetic to the plight of LGBTI refugees from other countries. He says Somali refugees faced the worst forms of harassment and discrimination thanks to their community's hostility towards homosexuality. The situation was made worse because they could not leave Kakuma and come to Nairobi, fearing police harassment, since all Somali refugees are now suspected of terrorism. And like the Burundians, Congolese and Ethiopians, the other big challenge for the Somalis was their inadequate grasp of languages beyond their local dialects, making it almost impossible for them to secure employment within the camp. The Ugandans who spoke English were employed to teach in the local schools within the camp. This, Wilberforce says, made things a little better for them.

Eventually, he was brought to the International Organization of Migration's (IOM) transit house in Nairobi. He says once he got here he wasn't allowed to leave until the time came for him to be taken to the airport. Everything was done for him – 'You are catered for,' he says. The transit house in Nairobi had beds, like a lodging, and Wilberforce stayed there for two days before being taken to the airport. There, as he waited to board his flight, alongside other refugees making the journey, Wilberforce was given snacks he could only have dreamt of in Kakuma.

Wilberforce's sense of relief is palpable over the phone, even a year later, from thousands of miles away where he is starting a new life.

I ask Wilberforce what it feels like to be in a new country away from the hardships of Kakuma, and now he can't talk. He tries to utter words but they are swallowed by huge sighs.

'It's a huge relief,' he finally says. 'It's such a huge relief.'

In March 2015, almost a year after Wilberforce had started his new life in a new country, a group of LGBTI Ugandan refugees and asylum seekers showed up at UNHCR's Nairobi office on Waiyaki Way in Westlands. They brought with them a memorandum of demands, telling UNHCR officials they wouldn't vacate the premises unless their demands were met. When the UNHCR wouldn't budge, the Ugandans brought out blankets and spent the night outside in the cold. The following day Kenyan police were called in. The Ugandan refugees say they were manhandled by both the police and UNHCR security guards, who were trying to make them vacate the premises.

In their detailed memorandum, the Ugandans claim the Kenyan government had informed them that they did not qualify for asylum and that they were only being granted refugee status on 'exceptional' grounds. This, they said, was because the Kenyan state was trusting that the UNHCR would quickly get them all out of the country as soon as they received refugee status, since homosexuality is illegal in Kenya.

In other words the Ugandans were claiming the Kenyan state was giving them refugee status only as long as UNHCR would speedily and automatically resettle all of them. Among the things UNHCR told the Ugandans[6] was that resettlement to third countries was not guaranteed and, even if it came, would take longer than imagined – up to three years – since a series of interviews had to be conducted at different stages. Resettlement was not a right but a privilege. The other heartbreaking piece of information, especially for newly arrived Ugandans, was that the duration between successive appointments on determination of refugee status and other UNHCR procedures was going to take months, due to what the UNHCR called lack of capacity. There wouldn't be any financial assistance since most Ugandans had outlived the three-month period during which UNHCR supports new arrivals.

Christopher,[7] one of the Ugandan refugees living in Nairobi (where he migrated after life in Kakuma got unbearable) claims the UNHCR is picking on Ugandans, and unfairly so. He tells me the UNHCR, through Hebrew Immigrant Aid Society (HIAS) Kenya, its

---

6 This was partly contained in 'The Updated UNHCR 5 Key Messages 2015'.

7 Names have been changed to protect their privacy.

NGO implementing partner, had promised them a monthly stipend of 6 000 Ksh each for as long as they were in Nairobi. Christopher had previously worked as a teacher, earning 5 800 Ksh per month, before he lost his job in a controversy about his sexuality. The new stipend was introduced after he was deemed to be part of an at-risk group, unable to work. But after receiving the money for a few months they were told they should each present a business proposal to the UNHCR, which would be seed-funded with 20 000 Ksh. Christopher says this was impractical, since not all Ugandan escapees are business minded.

'What if the business fails? Out of three hundred, ten may succeed. Then what happens to the rest? Will they go back to receiving the 6 000 or will that be the end of the road?' he asks.

About the protest at UNHCR in Nairobi, of which he was a part, Christopher has no apologies.

'Twenty of us decided we were going to sleep at UNHCR. Others were scared. We slept there. UNHCR asked for our file numbers. The guy who took them didn't return. We were hungry. We didn't have transport to go back home. We were told to go back to HIAS and do an assessment. We told them we had done our assessments already. So we slept at UNHCR. UNHCR only acts when you push them. People wrote to Geneva the other time. That is how things started moving. Should we write to Geneva again or should we wait for Obama?' he asks.

But that's not the end of the battle between the UNHCR and the Ugandans.

Part of a UNHCR document[8] asks the Ugandans, like all urban refugees, to be discreet and not blow their cover as LGBTI refugees and asylum seekers. But Christopher feels the UNHCR has become unreasonable, saying it has asked them not to have sexual relationships with anyone outside the group of Ugandans, because if they do they will be exposing themselves to risk.

---

8   This is partly contained in 'The Updated UNHCR 5 Key Messages 2015'.

'It is natural to have feelings,' he says, 'it doesn't matter whether one is Kenyan or Ugandan or Somali. It is normal to get attracted to someone. And if I am attracted to someone and I have the courage to approach them then I will do so. I don't understand how UNHCR can say I shouldn't when I will be in Nairobi for the next two years. Or am I supposed to live a confined life?' he asks.

Then, in tears, Christopher tells me a part of his story which he says he hasn't used in his asylum-seeking application because it may not be politically correct or sexy enough to have him granted refugee status. His mother was a Muslim when she married his Christian father, and eventually converted to Christianity. Years later, when his family got to know that Christopher was gay, they blamed his mother. They argued that her son's supposedly deviant sexual orientation was a punishment for her abandoning Islam. The resulting friction strained his parents' marriage so much, he says, that they eventually parted ways.

Christopher still blames himself for his parent's divorce.

Christopher's mother remarried and had more children – his younger sisters. For a brief period, life seemed liveable once more. His stepfather sent him and his sisters to the best school money could buy in Kampala, and his mother looked happy again.

This brief period of calm was shattered when Christopher's stepfather passed on, leaving the family in limbo.

Being just over 25 years old and having been in Kenya for the last four years trying to pursue his resettlement, Christopher considers himself 'a total failure'.

Tears flow freely when Christopher talks about his sisters going without food and his mother being an outcast. He tells me he blames himself for putting his mother in her current state, for ruining her marriage to his father and for not being in a position to support her now that she is a widow.

He wipes his tears and tells me he can't go back to Uganda in this empty-handed state.

Conversations in Kenya

In the eyes of some, the situation for LGBTI people in Kampala has indeed deteriorated. The first sign of deterioration was when leading local tabloids published the names of suspected gay Ugandans. The outing by tabloids put the lives of those mentioned at risk, making some leave Uganda and seek asylum elsewhere. Soon after the tabloid scandal, the Anti-Homosexuality Act (2014) was passed, criminalising same-sex relations. The Act included life imprisonment and penalties for individuals, companies, media/other organisations supporting homosexuals. Although it was later overturned by the courts, it created an environment of hate. The Act generated an atmosphere of fear and insecurity for sexual minorities thanks to the high political temperatures raised both inside and outside Uganda, and it is no coincidence that it was in 2014 – after the passage of the bill – that the number of Ugandans crossing into Kenya increased markedly.

UNHCR points out that there are 13 million refugees spread across the world – with over 586 000 in Kenya as of May 2015 – and that only 100 000 of the global refugee population can be resettled annually, a mere 7–8%.[9]

According to Eva Camps, a senior UNHCR protection officer based in Nairobi, someone must have misled the Ugandan refugees and asylum seekers in Nairobi who are now demanding financial assistance and the fast tracking of their resettlement, which they should know isn't guaranteed. She reiterates UNHCR's procedures – which she says the Ugandans have been made aware of time and again. Asylum-seeking is a long and tedious journey. The UNHCR is bound by rules and procedures within which it must operate – regardless of the fact that exceptions were made for the earlier arrivals from Uganda.

The same message is reinforced by George Onyore, a legal officer

---

9   Data provided by Eva Camps, Senior Protection Officer at UNHCR, Nairobi.

from HIAS Kenya. George says there are hundreds of other vulnerable urban refugees and asylum seekers, aside from the Ugandans. They include unaccompanied minors, the terminally ill, the elderly, and so on. For this reason, he says, the scarce resources shared between HIAS and UNHCR have to be used sparingly. HIAS does a continuous assessment of the needs of all refugees and asylum seekers. Based on this assessment, specific assistance is given to individuals who are found to be most needy. He reiterates: blanket assistance cannot be extended to the Ugandans.

Rachel Levitan, associate vice president of Global Programs, Strategy and Planning for HIAS has worked on the issue of LGBTI refugees and asylum seekers for close to seven years. She underscores the point others have made, which is that refugee protection, assistance and relief are not simple processes. She notes that these have been further complicated by the unexpectedly high refugee flows of the past five years. Furthermore, she says that in the case of Kenya the granting of asylum is delayed by increased security concerns – the larger context of Al-Shabaab and other terrorist groups. Aside from the urgent need for funds to cushion all at-risk refugees, including LGBTI asylum seekers, Levitan says there's always need to safeguard both the refugees and asylum seekers alongside their host communities, to diffuse inevitable tensions and incidents between the two.

For Eric Gitari, executive director of the Kenyan National Gay and Lesbian Human Rights Commission (NGLHRC), the situation faced by the Ugandans is dire. Yet he says that unless the Ugandans understand the predicament they are facing, it won't be easy bailing them out. Whatever UNHCR's shortcomings, he says, at the end of the day the Ugandans have to work closely with whoever is trying to assist them. He says the Kenyan LGBTI movement plays a double role as both a partner to UNHCR and a support for the Ugandans. Sometimes they advocate for the Ugandans by pushing their case with UNHCR; sometimes they play on the side of UNHCR in reiterating its positions to the Ugandans.

While it is tempting to see the asylum seekers as impatient and entitled, their predicament has real structural roots. A report, by Yiftach Millo, entitled 'Invisible in the city: Protection gaps facing sexual minority refugees and asylum seekers in urban Ecuador, Ghana, Israel and Kenya' points out that the needs of LGBTI asylum seekers are often invisible because it is near impossible for them to quantify their exact level of urgent need.

The report argues, 'Although the United Nations High Commissioner for Refugees (UNHCR) has made significant strides in its headquarters and in some country operations to protect sexual minority refugees, protection in the field remains extremely limited. Their protection is affected by a general misconception of lack of need and urgency resulting from the "invisibility" of their plight.'

Adrian Jjuuko, executive director of the Human Rights Awareness and Promotion Foundation (HRAPF) – the leading LGBTI litigation organisation in Uganda – says the majority of Ugandan LGBTI asylum seekers and refugees find it hard to quantify and then qualify what is considered persecution. This is because persecution is a deeply personal experience, and sometimes what passes as persecution in an individual's life might not hold water when they are subjected to legal rigours. This has led to many escapees forging documents, including warrants of arrest, which, when referred to his organisation for verification, are often found to be fake. This doesn't mean the escapee using fake documents was never persecuted, only that their true story of persecution might not be electrifying, and so they seek alternative narratives.

Some Ugandan LGBTI refugees and asylum seekers feel comfortable telling their secrets to Makerere University's Dr Stella Nyanzi of the Makerere Institute of Social Research (MISR), who they simply call Mama Stella. Dr Nyanzi says things get tough, especially for transgender women. They tell her they want to go to the market and buy a skirt, but this is impossible to do in Kenya because how do you even try on the skirt? So they do it when they sneak back into Uganda. In Uganda they know their way around. Similarly, they will sneak back to Uganda to try and find work because making a living in

Kenya is harder for them than in Kampala – or because the food they can afford in Kenya is terrible. Sometimes, she says, having that skirt can mean feeling dignified. These are the details that get overlooked; that bureaucracies cannot truly 'see'.

In the meantime, many Ugandans remain holed up in the slums of Nairobi, where they live illegally. The Kenyan government recently ordered all urban refugees to relocate to refugee camps due to the suspicion that Somali refugees were harbouring members of Al-Shabaab. UNHCR says this creates a precarious security situation. There are over 52 000 refugees and asylum seekers currently residing in Nairobi.

On the morning of 19 April 2015 the world woke up to news of the death at sea of over 700 Africans whose vessel capsized off the Libyan coast. They were on their way to Europe. On Twitter, a user asked, 'How do you face the Mediterranean and still decide to forge ahead?' #Africa was his hashtag of choice.

One might ask the same of the Ugandans.

Why do they live in deplorable conditions in refugee camps, knowing resettlement isn't guaranteed, or that if it comes it might take up to three years? Why do they squeeze into cubicles in Nairobi slums, hoping for survival money when there are no guarantees it will come? Why do they choose to face their particular Mediterranean?

In the case of Uganda the answers are complex. It seems as though many in the society will tolerate LGBTI people but will not let them live as freely as they need to live. It is obvious that those LGBTI people in Kampala whom I saw dancing and partying on my first night were able to do so because they are rich and protected or have mastered a method to manoeuvre their way around the homophobic society. On the other hand, the ones who run often do so after having been traumatised, or because, as Stella Nyanzi pointed out, they can't hold up their heads in dignity.

In the end, perhaps no one captures their predicament better than Somali poet Warsan Shire in her poem 'Home'.

Those who can afford to stay may not fully understand that, for some, leaving feels like a mater of life and death. At the same time, those who leave may not understand why their fellow community members choose to stay. And in the middle of all this, the UNHCR, the NGOs, and the complex system designed to facilitate asylum are clearly struggling to understand that many things can be true at the same time; that in fact home may tolerate you, but if it also forces you to negotiate your full humanity, then you'd rather live in limbo, in a camp somewhere, holding out for what is possible.

Scene of the crime

JACO BARNARD-NAUDE &
PIERRE DE VOS

This performance piece for two voices was written by Pierre de Vos and Jaco-Barnard-Naude as a site-specific, creative non-fiction work, performed at the remnants of Graaff's Pool in Sea Point, Cape Town on a chilly day in 2016. It formed part of the programme of the symposium Queer in Africa: The Cape Town Question. The authors engage with questions of race, gender and queer space(s) in contemporary Cape Town. Dialogically, the piece is a continuation of an earlier text which was performed at a conference in Stockholm, Sweden and later published as Barnard-Naudé and De Vos (2014) 'These queer gardens: a South African story', Acta Academica, 46(3): 134–150.

Scene: Graaff's Pool, Sea Point Promenade, Cape Town. Voice 1 and 2 are sitting in camping chairs.

1. ANTI-SOCIAL

Voice 1

[gazing into the middle distance]:

...as I was saying in Stockholm the last time when we talked about Koos Prinsloo: the queer erotic relation in his work is always close to death, the dying, the corpse. I mean, it's almost too obvious, calling a book *Slagplaas* and all that. And then there is the *Slagplaas* story itself, fuck, if ever there was a story of sex and death ...

[As s/he turns to Voice 2]:

You described the book as 'a volume of short stories about AIDS, sex, loneliness, the oppressive workings of heterosexual, white power in apartheid South Africa and the struggle with the real and symbolic father.' The struggle, then, with the figures and figurations of death. Because, you don't have to have read Lacan to know that the only good father is a dead father.

[Becoming agitated]:

It sounds anti-social, doesn't it? But let's not forget that for Freud, society as such is constituted in and through not simply the peaceful death of the father, but indeed his violent (some would say barbaric) murder. No wonder Walter Benjamin thought that there is no document of culture that is not at the same time a document of barbarism. So, to come back to Prinsloo, wouldn't you agree that his work really amounts to a profound destabilisation of these easy metaphysical opposites – life / death, human / animal, society / barbarism? I think that Koos Prinsloo, writing in the apartheid eighties, was well ahead of Lee Edelman's 'anti-social thesis', which has become so *à la mode* in American queer theory.

True, Edelman explicitly agitated for queer bodies to embrace the death drive, to radically subtract themselves from the social and political order, to fuck everyone and fuck everything, because the political is constitutively (and for him inescapably) the order of heteronormative compulsion. But isn't this exactly what Prinsloo's promiscuous characters enact time and time again? For Edelman, constitutive heteronormativity is exemplified in what he calls 'reproductive futurism' – the idea that society and politics is always already heteronormative, because it concerns itself with the future-as-reproduction of itself, with the children ('suffer the little children…'), and hence, with life. And I think it's the same for Prinsloo – he's not interested in a future as a reproduction of the Same.

[On a roll / strident]:

I have my reservations about Edelman's version of queer theory, as I have my reservations about Prinsloo. Edelman sounds a lot like a privileged, white, American man looking for an anti-political (and thus *political*) backing for apathetic resignation and the limitless *jouissance* of late capitalist subjectivity. So, trying to be 'radical', while, at the same time, also 'cool' – the having-your-cake (I almost said something else) and-eating-it pathology of the millennial subject.

[Suddenly unsure / tentative]:

But here we are in 2018 in Africa in Cape Town, talking about queer again, placing a suggestive question mark behind 'Queer Africa?' It seems to me that queer is very differently tied to death here. Or is it? Let's not forget that it's in the very same America of the anti-social thesis that a gunman still walks into a queer club and massacres 49 people – anti-social indeed. And that feels very close to home, in fact just a few blocks from here, just a few years ago, when gunmen walked into Sizzler's massage parlour and executed nine people … That was 2003, but it's not as if queer life has since become any less precarious: David Olyn, Eudy Simelane, need I go on? Bring it even closer to home? There is the story about you, M, another night club and, well, a sort of death … Or am I being too morbid here this morning at Graaff's Pool, where the ghosts of life, love, longing and pleasure seem to float, carefree, on the breath of the sea?

2. ANTI-RETROVIRAL

Voice 2

[almost melancholic]:

Ag, as you know the story of M was (or is – perhaps M and I are yet to write the last pages of this narrative) a very South African story, one about race (as all South African stories in one way or another always are), and humiliation and, perhaps, also an affirmation of life, a story written against the spectre of death. But which part of the story dare I tell? Is any part of it mine to tell at all? Or should I leave it to M, who has remained largely silent through all of this? As always, the problem of power – who speaks, who is heard, and to what end – presents itself, as Michel Foucault would have reminded us if he were still alive. The same Foucault who reportedly said in the hospital, while lying on his deathbed, ravaged by AIDS: 'You always think that in a certain kind of situation you'll find something to say about it, and now it turns out there's nothing to say after all.'[10]

But I am not dying. Or, perhaps, I am dying slowly, like all of us are slowly dying from the moment we are born. This, I am almost certainly only saying because I came across Michel de Montaigne recently and this line captured me: 'To philosophise is to learn to die'? He goes further. He says, 'To begin depriving death of its greatest advantage over us, let us adopt a way clean contrary to that common one; let us deprive death of its strangeness, let us frequent it, let us get used to it; let us have nothing more often in mind than death ... We do not know where death awaits us: so let us wait for it everywhere .... To practice death is to practice freedom. A man who has learned how to die has unlearned how to be a slave.'

[Cheering up, momentarily]:

And so, I have a lot to say, not so much about death, but about life. Not so much about the murder at Sizzler's which happened in a year to which

---

10 A. Ryan 'Foucault's life and hard times' *The New York Review of Books*, 8 April 1993, p. 17, quoting Herve Guibert's lightly fictionalised book entitled *To the Friend Who Did Not Save My Life* (Quartet, 1991).

we shall come back later. But about this promenade in front of us, with its muscled young men playing soccer on the grass, the families coming from far and wide to picnic, the lovers dancing to jazz near the ice cream kiosk during the summer months. And the memories of a walking wounded man wandering up and down this path, just here in front of us.

The story goes like this:

The man is sitting on the couch in the front room of the house that the man shares with M in Sea Point. The man nervously wipes the sleep from his eyes. Or maybe he is just fidgeting with his hands because he is anxious about what is to come. The smell of shit from his most recent bout of diarrhoea lingers on his fingertips. He wonders whether M can smell the shit from where he is perched on the armrest of the chair nearest the door, ready to flee to freedom. M is wearing the yellow and green Havaianas the man brought back from a recent trip to South America.

M has the habit of placing his hand in front of his mouth when he laughs in order to hide his teeth. Sometimes M casts his eyes to the floor in a manner that suggests an unspoken and immense hurt which remains largely unfathomable to the man – yet another divide that seems impossible to cross. M is not in the mood to laugh this morning. His left leg bops up and down as he speaks. 'I can't go on like this,' M says, 'because of what you have done to me. Because of everything.' The virus coursing through the man's blood remains unspoken. Also unspoken – but ever present in the room – the acts with other men, the acts that infected him (perhaps it was with the Salvadorian in the steam baths in Milan who jumped up after he came and burst into tears because in the next room the television – which usually shows men fucking in the most outlandish ways – was turned to the news where it had just been announced that the Pope had died?).

M stares out of the window towards the frangipani tree in full bloom, looking bewildered and trapped, yet somehow still performing stoicism and invulnerability. Maybe he is not staring at the frangipani tree but at something else – maybe at the white neighbours, just visible across the security wall, pottering around their small garden, perhaps.

Or at the black woman in a uniform (the type rich white people make their servants wear) pushing a white child in a pram? In any case, M is definitely not looking the man in the eye when he speaks. 'I have to go,' he says. There are no tears. The man jumps up from the couch and rushes past M. 'Sorry,' he says, then dashes to the toilet. It is the diarrhoea – even more than his heart – that propels him.

> *[Pause – a tear wiped away with the back of the hand; Voice 1 breaks eye contact and stands from the chair. He starts to move away]:*

By the time the house is turned over to estate agents every Sunday, the man no longer rushes to the toilet to shit: anti-retroviral drugs. Rather than deal with the unspeakable agent, the man wanders in a haze on the promenade. He picks at his own shame in those walks. Always, he returns home with only a vague memory of the afternoons. The taste of regret fills his mouth. The house is quiet and empty. The 'For Sale' sign on the front gate tells its own story. The bare stubby branches of the frangipani tree cast melancholy shadows over the stoep.'

> *[Exit both.]*

3. THE NAME OF THE PLACE WAS CAPRICE!

Voice 1

> *[enters reading from* The Flâneur: A Stroll Through the Paradoxes of Paris *by Edmund White]:*

Imagine dying and being grateful you'd gone to heaven, until one day (or one century) it dawned on you that your main mood was melancholy, although you were constantly convinced that happiness lay just around the next corner'.[11]

> *[Gazing into the middle distance again, as if remembering something; drops the book which will remain on the ground,*

---

11 E. White, *The Flâneur: A Stroll Through the Paradoxes of Paris* (Bloomsbury, 2001), p. 50.

blowing in the wind, for the rest of the scene]:

It was on one of those perfect, windless, lazy, sunny Friday afternoons in Camps Bay – one of those afternoons that the Western tourists jump on planes for, what they are prepared to buy with hard currency. In some sections of Cape Town society it was what is known as a 'laaifstaail' afternoon.

It was on one of these afternoons that he told me. It was not that I didn't suspect that something was amiss. But I was in the seductive thrall of wedding preparations, absorbed in the narcissism of knowing that I was going to be one of the first 'moffies' in South Africa to get hitched. And so, even though I wondered momentarily what was going on, I didn't pick up the phone. I sometimes still blame myself for that.

[Lights a cigarette while Voice 2 enters; continues, now addressing Voice 2]:

When you and M arrived on the farm that day for the wedding celebrations, I could see that you were unsettled. Your movement and your smiles were forced, at times even wooden. After the ceremony you congratulated me with tears in your eyes. Somewhere there is a photograph of you looking on at the dance floor...

Oh, how well do I know those melancholic shadows. Father Freud would have us know that melancholy is the intimate resurrection of the dead love object inside the ego. It is the refusal / inability to withdraw the libido from the lost one. Thinking about it now, is it heretical to say that you came to my wedding with death by your side, disguised in a fashionable drag of life?

[Passes the cigarettes to Voice 2, who also lights up]

That afternoon in Camps Bay was predominantly blue. Despite the technicolour cocktails that we drank one after the other sitting at the sidewalk bar, watching the noisy hodgepodge of overweight Europeans as they bumped up against Kodak Chinese, who sidestepped Zulu drum dancers stamping their feet under the tall palm trees.

You told me between the second and the third strawberry daiquiri, after I had told you about my exquisite honeymoon. First it was the diagnosis, then M's reaction. You told me about the symptoms, about how you thought you were dying before the drugs kicked in, about how in the bathroom mirror you stared death repeatedly in the face, only to be struck by an abandonment of life from another corner of the house.

[Puts out the cigarette, takes off his glasses and begins to wipe them on his shirt]:
Our friend from Australia, the psychoanalyst of children, once told me something that stuck. I was telling her about my childhood trauma, my youth killed by an alcoholic father and a mother who responded to years of abuse with an impenetrable psychosis, about living off peanut butter on white, government bread, about not having money for clothes.

She listened quietly to my complaint, which was also offered as a kind of explanation. Then she said: 'Have you ever thought about what it means that you survived?' At that moment, something changed in me. Until then, I always somehow believed that I had died in my youth, that something in me had been irretrievably lost and that it could never be regained; that the something was me, really. After that revelation, after she spoke those words, I think that I began to mourn for the first time, which is to say I realised that I was not dead, and that something indeed was lost forever, but that that something was not me.

[Joins Voice 2 and they start walking off together]:
This happened long after the afternoon in Camps Bay when you told me what I had not known. On that afternoon, I was lost for words. I said something inconsequential, something mechanical. My face tried not to give me away. I tried not to react as though you'd just informed me you had been given a life sentence. It was exceedingly hard. I am still not sure what my face managed to convey.

Nothing made sense and I was not expecting it to for some time. Still, when I looked up from the red mixture in my glass, I noticed the sign on the wall. The name of the place we were sitting at was 'Caprice!'

[Exit].

4. 'IT'S NOT RIGHT, BUT IT'S OK'

Voice 2

[singing along with Gloria Gaynor's hit song 'I will survive', playing from a portable speaker]:

...as long as I know how to love, I know I'll stay alive...

[Music fades out as Voice 1 enters wearing a feather boa, as if just back from a party; Voice 2 continues].

How many boys have I kissed at Bronx which was not so far from here, while this very song played and some twink or another with his shirt off gyrated around the pole fixed to the bar counter? Does the song resonate because the assumption has always been that as queers we are not likely to survive? Or that we shouldn't survive at all?

But some of us do not survive. The story of who gets to live and who gets to die, of whose lives are remembered and whose are forgotten long before they die, is also worth telling, don't you think? Is it possible to recount snippets – only half remembered and half understood – of one such life here? Perhaps? So another story. One that I have never told to anyone before. The story of R.

[Voice 1 and Voice 2 take their seats in the camping chairs again; Voice 2 continues].

The man met R on the promenade many years before he entered a relationship with M, long before anti-retroviral drugs started saving lives. It must have been a beautiful summer's night because R was wearing a pair of tight white shorts and white tekkies and a white T-shirt with the words: 'It's not Right, But It's Ok' printed in big black letters on the front. R was tall and skinny, with large dark brown eyes and a pair of perfectly straight rows of white teeth. He was chatting to his slightly chubby friend when the man spotted him. R was gesticulating wildly with his hands and was – long before Ru-Paul had made the term famous – sashaying along the promenade. Exuberant and playful, as if he was lovingly teasing his friend about something.

The man might have claimed that he was walking his dog when he met R, right here on the promenade. But that would not be true. The man had never owned a dog. It was at a time when the promenade was still a bustling cruising spot. Long before the City Council embarked on its own version of Operation Murambatsvina – a phrase from another context that stuck because everyone who doesn't matter doesn't matter in the same way. To be called trash – whether you are poor on the streets of Harare or queer on the streets of Cape Town, is to be rendered sub-human. Before the City Council decided to target the cruising moffies and the sex workers and the other undesirable elements (a code phrase for black people and poor people; for both?) in this area of town, long before the wall around Graaff's Pool was demolished, ostensibly to protect the safety of tourists who had begun to arrive in droves from Europe and America, and also, surely, to enhance the property values of the mostly white property owners in Sea Point.

No, the man was not walking his dog. He had recently come out of the closet and had heard that you could pick up men on the promenade. The man was a late bloomer and at the age of 31 – almost all of it spent celibate – he had a lot of sex to catch up with. R, still gesticulating, caught his eye and held it for just one second too long, then slackened his pace and, when the man tentatively smiled, broke away from his friend to introduce himself. Many years later the man cannot remember the details of what happened next, except that during the ensuing conversation, R at some point reached out and touched the man's arm. A reassuring gesture. Kind even. But also just a bit sexy. He must have noticed that the man was nervous and was about to flee.

Later, back in the Vredehoek flat, sitting still fully clothed on the mattress in his bedroom (there was no bed, just the mattress which the man – embarrassingly – thought rather bohemian), R laughed and said: 'You are such a frightened one, hey. Have you never fucked a man before?' In the conservative community from which the man came the word 'fuck' was only used as a threat – 'Fuck you' or 'I will fuck you up' – never as a description of desire or pleasure.

R, seeing the startled look on the man's face, smiled. 'You are adorable,' he giggled, before leaning in to kiss the man full on the mouth.

Later, still naked in bed, R told the man about himself. He had grown up in Hanover Park. His father was a pastor, of sorts, but he earned a living working as a packer in an ice cream factory. 'O jirre, 'n man van God,' R whispered and laughed, while absentmindedly tracing invisible patterns with his middle finger on the man's sweaty, hairless torso. R used to sing in the church choir – 'I used to channel my inner Whitney Houston in that choir,' R said. 'You can mos hear the gospel in all her songs.' He used to be close to his father, R said. Used to sit on his lap and play with his hair and talk about his day at Hanover Park High School, until the day, when he was 16 and he told his father that he liked boys. He was told to leave the house. 'Not a big scene,' R whispered. 'Daddy just got all quiet and hard and told me to leave.' R stayed at an aunt in Grassy Park for two more years until he wrote matric. Then he moved into a friend's house in town. The friend worked as an usher at the Labia theatre. 'Loves moffies, hey,' R smiled. 'She saved my life.' Now, said R, he worked in town at the men's clothing department of Edgars. R laughed again but it was a half-hearted kind of laugh. His mood had turned sad and he did not look the man in the eyes. 'No university for me,' he said. 'Not like you, Mr Clever.' He leaned over and kissed the man, as if to erase these last words.

The man saw R on and off for the next few months. R would call out of the blue and arrange meetings. R never gave his phone number – if he had one – to the man and they only met when R wanted to meet. When the man asked why he could not contact him, R just shrugged and said: 'I must keep you on your toes and keep you guessing.' They went on movie dates (R liked romantic comedies and his friend could sometimes smuggle them into the Labia), had ice cream on the promenade ('because,' said R, 'this is where we met – I am a romantic at heart, you know'), and spent nights on the mattress in the small room of the flat in Vredehoek. R never mentioned his father again. Instead he talked incessantly about pop music, but especially Whitney Houston. Late at night, lying naked in bed, used condoms neatly rolled up in toilet paper that R had collected before they went to the room, R would softly sing Whitney's songs. He seemed to know all the lyrics. 'Impossible'; 'I have nothing', and – later, deep into the night, his favourite – 'I will always love you'. 'But don't you get a big head now,' R said every time after singing 'I will always love you'. 'I am not singing that song for you. I am singing it for myself, hey.' The next morning, the man would drop R off at his friend's house in New Church Street, waving and smiling at R and waiting in the car until R disappeared inside the house. Then the man would drive to his office, the smell of R on his fingers for the rest of the day.

Then R stopped calling. After three weeks, the man worked up the courage and rang the bell of the house where he dropped off R. A woman in her mid-forties opened the door. She looked tired and a bit suspicious. 'No,' she said. 'There was no R living at this address.' Before the man could ask more questions, she closed the door. The man left. He assumed R did not want to be found.

He met N who worked at a publishing company. They embarked on a stormy relationship.

> *[Whitney Houston's 'I will always love you' begins to fade in from the speaker. Voice 2 grabs the feather boa from Voice 1, drapes it around his neck and waves its ends in the air.]*

It was filled with wild sex and wilder fights. It was all consuming. Except, sometimes, when he was dancing at the Bronx and a Whitney Houston song came on. Then, the man remembered R and wondered what had happened to him. He would dance some more though. Dance to forget

> *[Music now loud, plays for a few seconds, then stops abruptly. Voice 2 suddenly drops the ends of the feather boa and looks at audience, pause. Speaks softly]:*

More than a year after R had disappeared, the man bumped into R's friend at the Labia. 'Have you heard about R,' the woman asked. Before the man could respond, she continued. 'R passed away.' 'How?' the man asked. 'Why?' The woman shrugged her shoulders. 'Ag, let's not go into that,' she said. 'What would it help in any case.' Then she shoed the man into the darkened cinema. He took his seat to watch *Romeo and Juliet* – the Baz Luhrmann version – the one starring Leonardo

DiCaprio. Whether the man cried when Leonardo killed himself at the end, the author cannot recall.

[Voice 2 exits.]

5. SLAGPLAAS REMIX

Voice 1

[sits up in the camping chair, addresses the audience urgently]:
The smell was overwhelming but only if you understand that 'overwhelming' can be an understatement. The truth is the smell was fucking everywhere. In the air of the room, in the pillows and the sheets, in the clean laundry and in the dirty laundry, in the curtains and on the door handle, in the nostrils and, finally, in the deepest darkest neural pathways of the brain. The One was lying on The Other One's side of the bed, not facing the body of The Other who was lying next to him, asleep. The Other One was on holiday in France. It was only The One and The Other in the smelly apartment in Green Point.

The smell woke The Other. That and the noise. Because by that time the whistles, thump-thumps and cheers from the Pride parade that had been coming down the street since 11:00 that morning had arrived at their doorstep and had found their way through the window. It was too hot to close the window. The Other thought that it would also make the smell worse. He was too fuzzy from deep sleep to figure out if the smell was coming from outside or inside the apartment. It did not take The One long to begin his usual sulking, going on about the capitalist *jouissance* (a word he heard in a lecture given by The Other) of Pride, it's compulsion for pleasure and celebration, its refusal to commemorate and mourn when there is so much to commemorate and mourn. But The Other could not concentrate on anything that The One was saying. Because of the smell.

It was then that The One underwent one of the sudden personality shifts that The Other had grown accustomed to during the course of their short *menage*. The One took his phone from his pocket and was soon talking in muted tones to one of his 'friends'. He spoke just loud enough so that The Other would catch snippets of the plans he was making and that they didn't include The Other. Then he said goodbye, put the phone down, leapt from the bed and started spraying Jean-Paul Gaultier *Le Male* all over his young, lean body (it only made the smell worse, thought The Other).

'Where are you going?' asked The Other, although he already knew the answer.

'I'm joining the parade and meeting up with friends afterwards. Don't wait up for me.'

With that, he flitted out of the room and slammed the door shut as though to add the missing exclamation point from his parting sentence, which had nevertheless sounded like an order. The One was gone. And so too the rapid-but-vapid critique of Pride, thought The Other. Now The Other was alone with the smell.

The story of how The (older) Other met The (younger) One is too familiar and worn out to tell. Suffice it to say that by the time The Other was left alone with the smell he had, in a sense, already given up on The One. All that was left now was the melancholic's refusal to let go. The Other had a long history of compulsion – the inability to give up on things that had clearly become poisonous.

> [Takes a small handheld makeup mirror from his pocket, looks in it.]

The Other looked at his own face in the mirror. He felt abandoned and bereft.

> [Takes mascara and lip gloss from his pocket and, looking into the mirror, applies liberally; pouts in the mirror before returning it to his pocket.]

Eventually, The Other left the apartment. As soon as he was outside, The Other realised that (as someone once put it in another story), the air was thick with the smell. The parade was long gone. Flat balloons and spilled streamers mixed with some confetti, flyers inviting you to after parties at clubs and the odd abandoned banner ('We're here, we're queer!') were strewn about the tar of the still closed street – the only evidence that something celebratory had passed on.

The Other made his way to Somerset Road and the Pride after party. There he saw The One (even at a distance clearly high on his drug of choice, cocaine) passionately kissing an almost exact mirror image of himself behind one of the mobile stages. While The One was fully dressed to the nines, his mirror image was not. The fairest of them all was wearing only Havaianas and swimming trunks – apparel that of course revealed more than it concealed, notably, his huge erection for which the trunks were clearly becoming rapidly too small as The One's lips moved down his mirror image's neck, torso and abdomen.

[Gets up from the camping chair]:

At that point the smell became too much for The Other. He found his way to the exit and ordered an Uber which took him to Three Anchor Bay where he momentarily thought about drowning himself like Ingrid Jonker, but didn't want to ruin his makeup. In the end, he walked along the promenade and mostly thought about two things. First, why he had always felt so uncomfortable at Pride. He concluded that it was because something was critically missing from the Pride parade and that he had sensed this every time because he had always been unable to suspend his critical faculties in a crowd, to 'Just Enjoy!', to stop the constant stream of running commentary in his head (which was also why he drank excessively for years). The something that was missing from Pride, he thought, was post-apartheid South Africa. The truth was, he thought to himself, that there was not enough Queer at Pride.

Then he thought about The One and remembered how his friend the continental philosopher told him years ago that 'The Other fucks you up'. He thought especially about how The One had said throughout their acquaintance (for they didn't really know each other) that while he loved The Other, he had been struggling with physical intimacy since adolescence. The One said that he felt that The Other was the only one who understood this. The Other thought that, at the very least, he tried.

All of that, thought The Other, now looked like it had been a massive, bare-faced lie from the beginning, a spectacular conjuring trick, a *folie à deux*, even, which had cost The Other dearly and would keep on costing him for many years to come. Indeed, he felt like the woman in one of those shows that he remembered from his TV-saturated childhood in the eighties, where a magician puts the beautiful assistant in a box on stage and then proceeds to cut her up by forcefully pushing enormous, sharp blades through the box. After showing the audience the severed parts of the lady in the box, the magician would of course put her back together again, unlike Humpty Dumpty. In his case, the trick had gone badly wrong, there was blood all over the stage, the magician had fled the scene of the crime and Humpty Dumpty really couldn't be put back together again. What was also true, however, was that The Other didn't know at all (perhaps quite like the woman in the box) how one quits the cruel *jouissance* of The One.

When he arrived on the other side of the promenade he called an Uber again to take him back to the empty apartment (where he would jerk off that evening as though he was attempting a resurrection). While he waited for the Uber, The Other recalled how, that afternoon, The One, just after he had told The Other not to close the window, said what he had sensed The One was going to say: 'I think the smell is coming from something that's died in here.'

6. 'THE HEART UNDER SIEGE'

[Voice 1 and Voice 2 are in the camping chairs again. They are wearing dark sunglasses.]

Voice 2

[dramatic]:
'The child is not dead/ the child raises his fists against his mother/ who screams Africa screams the smell/ of freedom and heather/ in the locations of the heart under siege.'[12]

---

12 From 'The child is not dead' (first published in Afrikaans as 'Die Kind') by Ingrid Jonker. Published in *Black Butterflies: Selected Poems of Ingrid Jonker* (Human & Rousseau, 2011).

There is a story which I have told many times now, the one which in its retelling, has been polished like a diamond, so that it has become smooth and shiny and hard. It was the year of the Sizzlers massacre – 2003. On one level, I think the story says so much about what is wrong with all these supposed queer events and spaces in this 'mother city', who treats some of its inhabitants not like a mother should treat her child, but more like R's father treated him after he came out of the closet.

The man always tells the story in the same way. The punchline stays the same. It happened in the early days of the man's relationship with M in what the man imagines was an altogether happier time. In the two years that they had been together, the man and M had fallen into certain habits not uncommon for middle-class white gay men at the time. They worked in the week and on weekends they frequented the 'strip' in Green Point and danced the night away. 'We work hard and play hard,' might have been a cliché that rolled off their lips from time to time. In December they met up with friends and planned costumes and attended the Mother City Queer Project – first the Toy Box (the man proudly sewed their father Christmas outfits), then Farm Fresh (in which they went as beauty queens from the farm: Miss Holfontein and Miss Koekenaap, where the man bumped into one of his students and gave her an awkward hug while holding on to his wig).

On New Year's Eve, they sat on the balcony overlooking Somerset Road and watched drag queens jumping onto the bonnets of the passing cars, screeching with laugher, while couples inside looked either startled or amused. Of course, on one or two occasions – once over a glass of wine at home, another time at a restaurant in Mouille Point where all the waiters were white students from UCT – they spoke about how these supposedly queer spaces were dominated by straight-acting white men, how the waiters tended to offer the wine list or the bill, not to M – who earned more money – but to the man, how the man tended to be served much quicker at the bar than M ever was.

Then (and this is where the man would always tell the story in the same way) one evening after dinner the two of them went to a new club called Sliver which had opened up in Green Point. The man, already slightly drunk from the bottle of wine at dinner, went inside while M chatted to a friend outside. It was only after the man had already ordered another drink and M had not yet arrived that he went outside, where he found M arguing with two muscled bouncers who were refusing to let M into the club with the excuse that he was not 'appropriately dressed'. M was wearing a pair of jeans he had bought at Banana Republic on a trip to the USA and a pair of formal shoes – not really his style.

The man, being a teacher of human rights law, insisted that they challenge the club and the bouncers about their racial discrimination in the newly established Equality Court. In the process the man and M lost some friends – those who insisted that they were imagining things, that this could not possibly be about racial discrimination, those who suggested (being clueless about the law never having stopped the privileged from having an opinion about it) that the club had a right to reserve admission and that no law could have been broken, and those who suggested that it was better to let bygones be bygones and not to hold any grudges. But the man insisted that they go to court. It was a matter of principle. Besides, he knew the law and he knew that they would win. The day after the court victory – an apology and R10 000 paid to a charity of their choice by both the club and the bouncers – a large picture of them (both with big smiles, leaning in to each other) splashed on the front page of the *Cape Times* under the headline 'Gay nightclub admits to racial discrimination'. That night M and the man went to a restaurant in Sea Point, and toasted their victory.

> *[At this point, Voice 1 and Voice 2 start getting up out of the camping chairs, fold them up, start to pack their things away and take off their sunglasses.]*

It is at this point of the telling that the man would usually slip a wry joke into the story to make a political point. 'And you know what was the most telling thing for me,' the man would say whenever he told the story, and he would pause for effect before continuing. 'On the night of the event, after confronting the bouncer, and after he pushed M and then me and told us to go home, I pointed a finger at the bouncer and called him a racist.' The man would roll his eyes. 'But the bouncer did not respond at all. But then I made the mistake of calling him stupid and that is when he punched me and I fell to the ground.'

The punch line always elicited a laugh. And it made the point well. But still it missed a point too.

I Google the incident – our names and the name of the club. Up pops the story that was published on the front page of the *Cape Times* on 11 February 2004. I skim through it and read the apology made by the owners:

Voice 1 and 2

[alternating ad lib, facing the audience]: 'We, the owners of the Sliver Bar, admit that M's exclusion on that night was based on his race, in contravention of the Promotion of Equality and Prevention of Unfair Discrimination Act. We also understand that the exclusion was deeply hurtful (and) affronted his basic human dignity, sending out a signal that he was less worthy of respect than other patrons. We sincerely regret this incident and we apologise unreservedly.'

Voice 2

[as they start to walk off slowly, stops]:

M is also quoted in the *Cape Times* story. It is only one paragraph, but still. It is his voice. I read on, momentarily stunned: 'Speaking to the *Cape Times* on Tuesday, M said: "I am very happy with the outcome of the case and am glad Sliver has agreed to change their admissions policy. I was not confident about winning the case and the entire process has been difficult for me. Racial discrimination is intensely personal and goes to the core of human dignity."'

Voice 2

[takes out his reading glasses and puts them on]:

So, what I now realise is that I have been telling the story wrong all along simply because I have been the one telling it. Who speaks? Who is heard and to what end? This is the problem of power and it is the problem embedded within all these loves and all these lives – including my own

> *[Voice 1 is off, Voice 2 turns to the audience, removes the reading glasses]:*

It's not right but it's ok
   I will survive
   in the locations of the heart under siege

> *[Exit].*

Full Moon

JAYNE BAULING

WHAT WERE WE EXPECTING OF retirement and our permanent return to the tribal trust?

Of course we have visited over the years. After all, it is the same village where we found each other so long ago; two small girls, barefoot and busy with adventures.

We have been together nearly all our lives. We were parted at times in our young womanhood, but we found ways and so we always found each other.

Knowing our village as we did, we did not expect the elders to make it easy when we placed our official papers into their hands. There were many delays. In fact, still now, Vutengi has not been granted her piece of ground. Her brothers and their families are busy hounding her about her intentions and making excuses. They want to find some unofficial way of claiming the land for themselves.

'You don't need it,' they say.

They are implying she doesn't need it because we are living together in the small house we built with our hands when the elders gave me my permission. Vutengi listens to her brothers, but says nothing. She hopes her children can benefit in some way when her land and building permission come through. She has a son and daughter, from one of the times of compromise, when her family made her marry a man.

I too have a child, but I don't know where he is. He came from my punishment. Today they call it 'correcting', or 'curing'. Back then they simply called it a punishment.

That was one of the bad times, and I was still sick in my mind and my body when the boy came, so they took him away.

Vutengi found me and healed me and made me strong, and I have never allowed myself to be broken again.

The house where we live is on the dark side of the hill. The only place where the elders saw fit to place us. We built it over many years. We spent many of our weekends off building this house. We both worked on the big paprika farm near Ohrigstad. After we retired, the farm rehired us on temporary contracts. Vutengi worked in the office and I stayed outdoors – working in the nurseries. The work was the same as we had done before.

Some building weekends we would arrive at the village and find parts of our house dismantled. Often there were materials missing, even though we were careful about locking everything away, and despite the fact that we had asked a young man to guard it for us. It did not deter us. We would simply begin again, determined to finish our house.

We live here now, enjoying the fruits of our labour. The only other building close by is a house someone started to build but didn't finish. Cement floor, and walls of grey blocks as high as my head, roofless. Perhaps whoever began ran out of money, or died, or became dismayed by the darkness on this side of the hill. Now teenagers sometimes use it to have sex they believe is secret.

The dark side of the hill makes us laugh. We have worked all our lives on farms. We know how to make things grow. Our vegetables are better than most grown on the other side; big and bright, as crunchy or tender as nature means them to be.

Some of the villagers think it is witchcraft that pushes our carrots up and makes our spinach so green.

So they shun us. The children especially like to pitch stones on to our roof.

'It would make me happy if they would just ignore us,' Vutengi says after someone kills the dog. 'We don't need them.'

We don't need anyone. We have each other, our pensions, and enough to eat.

We are not the villagers' business, but they make us so.

While we are waiting for Vutengi's land to be granted to her, they bother us every day.

First the elders come.

'You bring shame on us.'

The man chosen to speak will not look at us, and we are not supposed to look at him, but we do. He continues. 'You shame yourselves.'

'How?' Vutengi asks, facing them standing outside our house.

'This thing…' He cannot make himself name it.

'We are not ashamed.' I fold my arms across my chest. 'It is your problem if you are shamed. We cannot help you.'

Long ago we promised each other never to apologise. Apologies led to the times of compromise. To fictions and fronts, things done for appearances, and for the ease of others.

'This thing.' A second man tries to help the first. 'It comes from far away. From the city. Maybe from America and those places we see on TV. It is not a Tsonga thing.'

'But we are Tsonga – you watched us growing here,' Vutengi says.

'This provocation will not be tolerated,' the first man wheezes, leaning on his stick.

'Are you worried?' I ask Vutengi when they have left.

'Not me. Are you?'

'Not yet.'

Next they send the pastor. He hesitates when we invite him into the house. Then he enters, but refuses our offer of tea and biscuits.

'This thing…' he begins.

I am getting tired of that phrase.

Then he uses other words and phrases: *unnatural, the eyes of God, sin.* He speaks them quietly, but they are ugly.

I regret inviting him in.

He cites the Bible. Leviticus. Romans.

'We will pray for you,' he says on leaving.

'Use your prayer for those who need it,' I tell him. 'Don't waste it on us.'

The other pastor – the new one who holds long, loud services in the blue-and-white tent – will not even bother to contaminate himself with a visit.

We learn this from Vutengi's older brother, who comes sniffing to find out if her plot has been granted yet.

Apparently the new man trumpets against us on Sundays. We are an affront, an obscenity. We must be dealt with.

'He is getting people stirred up, telling them you are deliberately insulting them, flaunting … this thing.'

'This thing,' I repeat.

Vutengi and I look at each other, and share our secret smile.

'We don't care enough about them to want to do anything to them deliberately,' Vutengi says.

'A little humility, perhaps?' her brother suggests, holding himself stiffly.

'In place of honesty?' I ask.

He doesn't answer me. He simply turns and goes away.

From the beginning, the family blamed me for Vutengi. She minds this more than I do. Perhaps this is because it is her family.

'Who is next?' she wonders later when we are talking about the visits and the sermons.

The village is next. As she passes on her way down to the main road, a woman shouts that we are sick.

We are outside, taking advantage of the two or three bright hours when the sun touches our side of the hill. I am turning over a new stretch of ground for more vegetables, and Vutengi is weeding among the brinjals.

'We still need to get some chickens, Ritlatla,' she reminds me when the woman has gone. 'And we spoke about a goat ... What is wrong?'

She reads me like that.

'I am remembering the dog.' The old woman has loosed something in me.

She looks at me, and then dips her head. We both remember the bloody mess of the dog's dying body again.

After the woman there is a period of quiet. Then it begins again. The colours of our vegetables make a living calendar of the year's seasons.

Sometimes the colours disappear overnight, or there are gaps in the neat rows. They rip up seedlings, leaving them limp and drying on top of the scuffed soil.

There is no mistaking it. This is not hunger, it is spite.

We cannot hide it from ourselves. I see wetness in Vutengi's eyes. As for me, I am angry.

'If I was a young woman,' I threaten.

Pointless to say. I am not young. My arms and legs ache on many days. I am dried out of the oils and juices that made me such a strong worker. It is the same for Vutengi; her hands shake all the time now, and she drops things.

Still we cause offence.

They – always an unknown they, people with no names, only actions – throw waste at the walls of our house.

They break a window.

I think about getting another dog, but you never know how a dog will turn out, coward or killer.

Some days, the smallest children come to shout at us when we're in the house. They turn their taunts into chanting the way children sometimes do. They keep their distance – ready to run if we step out. When we do, they scream as they run, and we hear in their voices the terror and delight of little ones who know but do not know what they do.

The teenagers stare and snigger. Or they call out new words their generation have for us. They are words we have not heard before, although we have heard many other words.

Sometimes they are drunk. The calling gets louder then, and stupider.

A group comes by. They shout. There is fear in the way one boy looks at us. He looks as though he is no more than sixteen. He is strong and fit. I wonder, why is he so afraid?

Another regards us with open curiosity, and something like greed. He looks as though he is wondering what it is we do, and if we still do it, at our age.

The thought makes me smile, Vutengi too when I share it with her.

But we are smiling less these days.

'Go practise your depravity elsewhere, in the cities where they like your kind. Shameless women.' This time it is a man our age who shouts at us in a voice that quavers, the same way Vutengi's voice has started to.

My voice is still strong, but sometimes I struggle for words I used to find without thinking.

More seedlings are torn up. It happens in the night.

'Perhaps they hope to starve us off the hill,' I say when we find the molested path of earth in the dim early morning. I am not completely joking.

'We should keep watch.' Vutengi is shaking worse than usual. 'One of us at all times.'

We try, but we are at a time in our lives when sleep can fall upon us at any moment. And anyway, what would we do if we caught someone?

Another night, when we are both sure we haven't slept, we fail to hear someone peeing against our front door.

We cannot trust our own impressions of sleeplessness.

'Should we leave this place?' Vutengi is the first to say it.

'And let them believe they have driven us out?'

'We have fought so many battles, my love.' She sounds tired.

'You think this is the one we should walk away from?'

'It is the last one.' She is pleading. 'If we stay, we will always have this ... Our house spoiled, plants destroyed. They could hurt us.'

I hear that she is afraid. It is so many years since we have allowed ourselves to fear.

I press my lips together, looking at her and thinking.

'We need to think of a way to go that will say it was our own choice.'

Something that was bright is fading inside me.

All the ways I can think of are too dramatic. They involve harm, even destruction – acts that are beyond our strength now, and would make us like them.

We cannot rush this. As younger women, it was always easy for us to move on, never because we were defeated or afraid, but because we were tired of a place or disliked people who also disliked us.

So we plant more vegetables and try to guard them.

'It is full moon tonight,' Vutengi reminds me when they have been in the ground a week. 'They will come again, like last month.'

Last month, drunk teenagers' dancing and singing turned to wild laughter and screaming as they reached our house. Later, they partied the rest of the night in the half-built house next door that would have been a home to our neighbours.

We wait and watch, with no light in the house save the silver-ice glow of the great moon. A dog howls on the other side of the hill, but otherwise it is quiet, even the night birds silent.

'Perhaps they have something better to do this month,' I dare to joke, to hope.

'No, look.' Vutengi is out of her chair. 'There.'

I look up and see them; two figures, dark shapes in the moonlight slinking into the unfinished building.

'Only two,' I register, and I'm in the hold of something fierce and grim, something I thought the years had soothed. 'There for sex. Let's frighten them, give them a real reason to hate us.'

'Ritlatla?'

But Vutengi knows me in this mood, and she doesn't expect me to answer. She even smiles.

One last time, I'm thinking. Of course, two old women cannot match two teenagers, but in the moment of their fright we will hold the power.

We are quiet, but not silent, leaving the house. Vutengi wheezes slightly every few breaths, and I puff over upward-sloping ground.

The unfinished building is dull, moonlit but unreflective. From inside comes a scuffling, then something like a sob, and a groan.

We circle the place until we find the gap that would have been the door. Holding on to each other, we edge through it.

We must make some sound, startled by what we are seeing.

I recognise the lovers. It is the boy who looked at us with so much fear, and – skin gleaming in the moon's glare, half-naked in his arms, turning towards us and then frozen – the curious one. I see their terror. The fearful one begins to weep.

Vutengi and I look at each other. These boys are us, at our beginning, standing as we had at the dawn of our discovery of ourselves and each other.

We don't have to say it. The plan to move away is cancelled. We stay.

Sailing with *The Argonauts*[13]

EFEMIA CHELA

*Actually, no one is inspired by anyone except his own self and
his own anguish*
– EUGÈNE IONESCO[14]

CHRISTMAS IS MY STRAIGHTEST TIME of year and it is then that I read
Maggie Nelson's *The Argonauts*. I am bi but I have to be straight at
Christmas. It's someone else's Christmas wish. There isn't any other
choice. My parents are what I'd describe as Christian Fundamentalists.
Somehow I'm always at home to deck the halls (which we don't

13 Previously published in Issue 1 of *The Johannesburg Review of Books*.
   Available at: www.johannesburgreviewofbooks.com/2017/05/01/sailing-
   with-the-argonauts-a-personal-history-of-christmas-queerness-and-
   maggie-nelson-by-efemia-chela/ on 1 May 2017.
14 E. Ionesco, *Notes and Counter Notes: Writings on the Theatre*, translated
   by Donald Watson (Grove Press, 1964)

actually do to avoid the sin of excess), having boomeranged back there after my once bright and seemingly permanent plans for the year have failed again:

A Short History

2013: Retrenchment

2014: Severe depressive episode

2015: Not so big in Japan

2016: Can't remember. Won't remember.

My people are the people my parents make fun of on a good day, and revile and accuse of all manner of arbitrary evils on a bad day. According to my mother, Trump, Brexit and trans bathroom rights suggest the end is near. Jesus is coming and she can't wait to meet him.

We are at the mall and it is clogged with people taking selfies in front of a giant fake albino Christmas tree. It's baubled and tinselled. They are all getting in the way of each other. Stray arms and legs cross the borders of pictures in smartphones in front of the alien tree. The composition of each of their photos is disturbed but they carry on. This is a season in which nothing makes sense. When we are inside Edgars on our way to buy sensible underwear (which is fitting for an unmarried woman like me), not a present (because the commercialisation of Christmas increases Satan's power over us), I detour to the MAC counter. Aside from the pavements in front of local butcheries, where Afrikaans butchies with binding, board shorts and flat caps, slouch, this is the queerest part of Pretoria – or at least the most openly queer. I am delighted by the rows of makeup and the hope of non-heterosexual outlooks on life (read: gossip and sex tips).

My mother, out of her element under the bright lights, clubby music and makeup, refuses to be served by the queen in black pleather shorts *who's about to give her her goddamn life honey and make her face werk, girl with the best coral lipstick for her BAMF melanin das poppin'*.

Her face deflates like a collapsing bouncing castle. She clutches her handbag and leans away as her eyes bulge. I stand in front of her and pout, my eyes closed. I try the colour. I pretend I'm kissing a girl. I open my eyes and look in the mirror. There is no other girl there and the colour looks awful on me. My mother complains the whole car ride home. She continues to complain for weeks afterwards to everyone who will listen and especially those who won't.

When I cannot bear to hear the story again I go to my room, to *The Argonauts* by Maggie Nelson. The volume is slim but it contains multitudes. Completely genre-queer, it melds a letter to Harry, Nelson's lover with remembrances, polemic, philosophy and gender theory. All seamlessly. Densely packed, the book is a steady chapterless stream, each daring proposal and paragraph reaching for the next. The shoulders of the people Nelson stands on gird the margins, making endless further reading inevitable. This is a book of revelations.

Viewed from one angle, it is the story of Maggie falling in love with Harry and his transition from woman to gender fluid, leaning more male. Maggie also falls pregnant, discovering the double queerness in hosting a future person. The love between Maggie and Harry changes throughout the book, as their emotional, physical and physiological states are in flux. The book explores the social fear that permeates the idea that love changes. That the person you love may change, that your terms of commitment may loosen or tighten, that your own essence may shift and that with these changes automatically follows incompatibility and the death of love. The concept is less controversial than gay rights but it is almost as threatening, a phenomenon that society fears just as much. Thousands of songs are about perfect love being the same, never-changing, endless (that plastic Christmas tree). Static yet alive, ever fresh, like some sort of GM food. Maggie debates this and makes her truth, by way of Roland Barthes, clear early on – love will change and that is not wrong:

> [...] the lover utters the phrase 'I love you', its meaning
> must be renewed by each use, as the very task of love and of
> language is to give one and the same phrase inflections which
> will be forever new.
> – Roland Barthes[15]

Maggie makes the renewing of love sound not Sisyphean, but like a natural buffing and refining. A comforting habit, like massaging your scalp while washing your hair. Natural incidence. Things will roughen again. Your scalp will flake and locks will get oily and that is the point: there is growth, strength and pleasure in the repetition. This is love freed of an overarching goal.

Similarly, *The Argonauts* is free of grand expectations of what, as a book, it ought to be. Maggie's playfulness with form makes it feel like she isn't trying to lure us towards a neat conclusion. Is an overriding conclusion even possible if, in a mere 143 pages, the author journeys through life (the birth of her son, Iggy), death (of radical queerness and her mother-in-law) and her concern at the under-exploration of the female anus in criticism? After all, she says: 'My writing is riddled with such tics of uncertainty.' And it is this trait that makes the book so successful. Maggie's uncertainty triggers her universal questioning, which covers everything from the most complex ideas to the most fundamental: language.

The keel of *The Argonauts* is language: Maggie's wrestling with language; names of states of being; changing legal names; names people call you. Someone called me a writer, once. Someone said, writing is about putting into words things that can't be put into words, once.

---

15 Quoted in M. Nelson, *The Argonauts* (Graywolf Press, 2016). All further quotes are from *The Argonauts*.

> Before long I learned that you had spent a lifetime devoted to
> the conviction that words are not good enough. Not only not
> good enough, but corrosive to all that is good, all that is real,
> all that is flow. We argued and argued on this account, full of
> fever, not malice. Once we name something, you said, we can
> never see it the same way again. All that is unnameable falls
> away, gets lost, is murdered.
> – Maggie Nelson

Maggie's partner, Harry, expounds on the grand cruel irony of words. Once things are named, they lose their mystery and power. But until they are named, it is as if they do not exist. My experience as a bisexual femme is murdered out; I don't exist. I have long hair and visible breasts. With my lipstick collection, jewellery, skirts and lack of interest in sports, cars or carpentry, I pass as straight to most people. They don't have the right words for me as I don't fit into their bank of clichés. This is not the droid they're looking for

The framework of heteronormativity refuses to recognise 'queer' as 'perpetual excitement' – what Maggie describes as a swirling maelstrom of resistance against various forms of oppression, shapeshifting placeholder that includes all types of people, orientations, sexual preferences and struggles. Seldom is queerness depicted as gay, in the happy sense of the word and 'happy' queerness is something I don't get to experience often.

The general public, strung out on heteronormativity, assume I'm straight or just tell me I am, depending on how rude or how drunk they are. To stop my vulva from atrophying, I have to prove that I'm gay. Something that is tricky to prove, short of being given a bedroom, a recording device and access to another person's body (and still not a 100 per cent conclusive test). But even if I could prove I was gay, my reward for proving it would be reproach for being gay:

'You could bring so much disease into our lesbian community fucking guys as well. That's so selfish!'

'Seriously?! I feel like this is something you'll get over eventually.'

'I don't want to be dumped for a chick.'

'*Ebei*!!! This is a perversion only Jesus can heal. I know this is not your portion. O! *Eranom*! The blood of the lamb … abeg.'

'That's not a real thing. It's just a phase.'

'Greedy aren't we? Just pick one.'

When Harry starts taking testosterone, Maggie says, 'visibility makes possible, but it also disciplines'. So mostly out of convenience I fake straight and shut the queer part of my life away. Ironically, I am simultaneously desperate to be seen, and also to hide. I am hidden by my own mouth's silence. Garden variety homosexuals get to come out once. Any other queer has to convert the world over and over again. It is exhausting unpaid labour, often painful and futile:

> How to explain, in a culture frantic for resolution, that
> sometimes the shit stays messy?
> – MAGGIE NELSON

And that's before we've even addressed class or race or 'finding someone with whom my perversities are not only compatible but perfectly matched'. Sometimes when I walk past the white lesbians loitering outside the butcher's, and there's a woman I admire, I wonder – if we fucked would I be able to tell if it was BDSM or a lynching before it was too late?

I am mid-voyage on *The Argonauts* in the slide towards Christmas Sunday. I keep reading during small breaks in the preparations for a party I am increasingly nervous about. We will be 20 people in a small suburban house, being held to ransom in a heatwave. It's all a bit too Tennessee Williams, even for me – and I love Tennessee Williams. A gathering of people in forced gestures of celebration after a wretched year. We have two lacklustre marriages and one openly failed one. There is a dying family friend, the spectre of an absent father, a prodigal daughter (back from America). My halfployment and my cousin's anxiety join the party. There are two people with disordered eating, only two bathrooms, eleven individual dishes, and me to play host and pair wine with everything. It's fucked. I start chasing Valium with wine as soon as I brush my teeth. In literary fiction, terror is always portrayed as beautiful, but this is my life, reality, where terror is my beautiful face with my voice so sad and no one noticing.

I will always aspire to contain my shit as best as I can ...
– MAGGIE NELSON

When I read this quote, I am reminded of why I read. Reading allows me to be part of something, a community, even though I am almost always physically alone. Usually in bed. Some days the longest amount of time I spend out of bed is the thirty minutes it takes to eat something and falsely assure everyone in the vicinity that I am completely alive and okay. Reading allows me to hope to be better, to reach the state of self in the second part of the same sentence. Maggie continues. She wants to contain her shit yes, but that isn't all she wants

... I am no longer interested in hiding my dependencies
in an effort to appear superior to those who are more visibly
undone or aching.
– MAGGIE NELSON

I want to be more radically queer regardless of the consequences and because of the consequences. I want a dissipation of my current ennui, a better life for myself and a more flexible queer-friendly world. Any book that insists that both shifts, internally and externally driven, are possible, is surely a golden fleece. *The Argonauts* is more-than-memoir. It is a manifesto, a record, a dream – something big and real about living and loving in-between: in between life and death, male and female, law and lawlessness, love and indifference, language and ideas.

The family and guests gather. I think of chapped hands during prayer. Everything is a haze of food comas, festive lights and terrified pretending. I am losing myself in heteronormativity. The unsaid, triggers, offensive comments are deflected by blank stares and feigned deafness. I wake up hungover, dry-mouthed in bed on Boxing Day and can hear remnants of food congealing on dishes. I am 'undone' and 'aching' as much as anyone – maybe more than most. Still at least I know that I can always sail back into *The Argonauts*; I can re-join Maggie in her eternal quest. The ship awaits.

Taking a walk in Princess's shoes as she prepares for the Pretoria Parade

CARL COLLISON

A TINY ROOM IN A COMMUNE FILLED with a seemingly endless number of other small rooms is what Princess Selota calls home.

'I've only been living here three months,' says the 24-year-old, who is originally from Limpopo. 'My mom is in Jo'burg, but I hardly get to see her. But she loves me. I'm her little princess.'

Leading me into her sparse no-frills bedroom, Princess says: 'It's mainly nurses who live here. And also students studying at Steve Biko Memorial Hospital.'

A tall, lithe transgender woman with delicate features, Princess may not fit the archetypal image of a nurse. But as a peer educator for Wits Reproductive Health and HIV Institute she is a health practitioner.

She is setting out to meet colleagues going to this year's Pretoria Pride parade – 'to do some awareness-raising about the work we do,' she says, fixing her makeup.

About half an hour later, she slips into a sleeveless black top and long, floral skirt. After the long makeup-application session, the dress seems to take seconds to put on.

Stepping out of her room, we are spared the hassle of having to catch a minibus taxi (her usual means of travel) by a young man, a resident in the commune, who offers us a ride.

'Sisi, does your boyfriend drive?' he asks her as we walk toward the gate. He is on his way to treat his family to a day out, he says. 'Let me drive you … seeing as it's so cold,' he offers.

'He doesn't know my gender,' she says after he drops us off. 'And he thought you were my boyfriend.' We laugh.

We meet the other peer educators on the street outside their offices in central Pretoria. Standing in front of a Christian bookstore selling all manner of Bible-based paraphernalia, the gaggle of transgender women and straight-looking queer boys are a mixture of nerves ('we're not going to get there on time') and raucous laughter ('hawu, we saw her with a man last night, now she wants to say she's sick?').

The group of eight – boys in functional jeans and T-shirts; girls teetering in bright, kick-ass heels — stick out like a beautiful, defiant sore thumb among the throngs making their way to work or running early-morning errands.

During the taxi ride, the latest gqom tracks blast furiously. 'This one makes everyone lose their morals,' one of the boys laughs and everyone laughs with him.

Arriving at the Centurion Rugby Club, where the Pride march will end and a hodgepodge of stalls are being set up, it turns out the stress of not getting there on time was somewhat misplaced. The girls have time to slip into their tutus.

After decorating the mobile clinic with balloons and ribbons ('the mobile clinic looks so gay today,' someone quips), Princess and her crew set up their gazebo. This will serve as their base camp for their awareness-raising activities. Amid much laughter, they set about packing gift bags containing everything from lubricant and condoms (male and female) to multivitamins.

Occasionally, Katlego Serame, the project's team leader, starts twerking. She is roundly applauded. 'I can twerk, too,' she says. 'Trans women can twerk.'

'We have a really strong bond,' says Princess of her fellow peer educators. 'We are sisters now. We call each other family. I learn a lot from them.'

Tent set up, we decide to head to the bar while we wait for those marching in this year's parade to make their way into the park.

'Oooh, I love pink drinks,' she says, sipping on her fruit-flavoured cooler while simultaneously bemoaning the exorbitant prices. 'It makes Pride feel like just a money-making thing. But still, it brings people together.'

Sipping lazily on our drinks, we stare at the revellers slowly making their way into the park. Many of them are couples walking hand-in-hand, probably grateful for a space to demonstrate their affections. Princess looks at a couple wistfully. 'You know, sometimes you need someone. My relationships never last. I don't know if it's me,' she laughs, self-deprecatingly. 'Like today. It's such a lovely day. You want to go home and be able to share that with someone.'

She is interrupted by another burst of laughter from her sisters. She smiles as she stares at them – Serame, the group's witty, jaw-droppingly beautiful and confident mother figure and Kinnah van Staden, the warm-eyed, soft-spoken observer. Princess comes back to our conversation though. She may not have someone at the moment, but she adds, 'But I'm happy. Me, I'm always happy.'

* * *

See photo essay, pp 161–69.

Africa's future has no space for stupid black men[16]

PWAANGULONGII DAUOD

Boy, that night was energy.

It was the night that I'd last see C Boy, for a couple of weeks later, in March, he would be found dead in his backyard. The night was full of energy. The kind of energy that Africa needs to reinvent itself. Fierce. Electrifying. Full.

13 January 2015. On the second anniversary of the day and year Nigeria signed the anti-gay bill into law, I honoured an email invitation from C Boy to attend a secret party for homosexuals he was hosting in a nightclub in Kaduna. The invite mentioned coming along with a

16 Previously published in *Granta* magazine, 13 July 2016

partner who had enough discipline to keep a secret. 'The partner may be "straight" but must not be homophobic; an artist is preferable,' it emphasised. And beneath it was an NB that read: 'There will be a brainstorming session on the word AFRO-MODERNISM. We are giving it a new meaning. Kindly pre-study the word.'

It sounded like a great idea, so I called a lesbian friend (a photographer-cum-designer-cum-blogger) and we headed to the nightclub somewhere in Kaduna South, known as Barnawa.

C Boy was from Adamawa. His father had sent him to Zaria to study Engineering at the Ahmadu Bello University, because he 'wanted his family to produce the first engineer in his hometown'. But C Boy had another plan; on arriving in Zaria he deferred his admission, rented an off-campus flat, and began learning software applications, website creation and concept development, all by himself. He was doing this until the next session when he began his classes. But still, he wasn't excited. Most of the times, he was out of Zaria, travelling by night bus to far away Port Harcourt to visit his lover, a boy he had met and fallen in love with through Facebook just before he was given admission. 'My father was thinking I was the "obedient" budding engineer from his hometown. But leaving his house was leaving his ways and dreams. Everyone got his drives. My father's is not mine,' he said to a group of students in his apartment one Sunday morning in 2013. We were having a Sunday brunch.

It was from his numerous visits to Port Harcourt that he found a gay community and thought of founding one himself in Zaria.

11 pm. We arrived late. A friend dropped us off a street away from the club, and we begged him to return for us at five in the morning. He drove off, and we crossed the road to our destination. My partner led the way to the nightclub; I walked behind, carrying her camera, a notepad and a spare pullover. The harmattan was a bitch.

I swear. The bouncers at the doorway would scare the hell out of John Cena. They allowed us entrance when we showed an e-copy of the invite on my friend's phone.

There was a check-in desk in the hall. We were issued tags. Mine read,

We are the Future Democracy, and hers, **In Our Father's House, There are Many Loves. We Chant It Cos Its So**. Soon we walked inside to join the party.

C Boy, our host, saw us from where he was standing by the DJ booth and started towards us, smiling. His jeans, dyed dreadlocked hair and dashiki matched the colour of wine in the glass in his hand. Burgundy.

The party pulsated. It was a festival of energy, of music, of hair, of ideas, of gays, of happiness, of fashion. Of language, love, meaning. A festival of dreams and assertion.

My partner headed to the bar for a drink, and I jumped to the dance floor to rock lost-but-found folks and long-time brothers.

I first met C Boy on 14 September 2012. He had been invited to perform at a poetry slam I was hosting on the rooftop of a house in Samaru, Zaria. Apart from stealing the show with his epic spoken-word performance, he fought with a guy who had performed a poem that mocked homosexuals. He was mad like a bull that night. He would have killed the guy if not for the crowd that fought to restrain him. After the event, I recall, he sat apart from everyone in a yellow plastic chair, and wept like a child. We became friends and soon started getting to know each other: I am bisexual, he's homosexual.

C Boy was the engineering student who could recite all the scholars in the humanities and their theories by heart. He read the postcolonial texts, and hated Walter Rodney. It was through rumour I found out that he had dropped out. 'Yes, I left engineering,' he told me 'It wasn't a dropout, it's a change over.'

Cliché, but the true nature of things: If you are found to be gay in Nigeria, you are on your way to prison to rot away for the next six hundred and something weeks of your fucking life. And that's through sheer luck. Because you don't always get it, you can't always get it. Why? Because you are the demon that needs to be exorcised, lynched, stoned to death, hacked to death, burnt to death, beaten to death, or done something to to death. It doesn't matter how: you must die, before the law manages to stroll by to see your predicament. So, to avoid rotting away in prison or getting killed you take to secret love and/or a pretend heterosexual orientation.

It was to re-interrogate this narrative that C Boy dropped out of school. It sounded like a crazy and risky idea for a 24-year-old to be leaving school for such a project, but C Boy had guts. All he wanted was to found a club that served LBGT people, a space where they could network and find expression. A warm brotherhood for people of 'like passions' living in a society that demonises them. 'The club has to be an energetic underground space,' he once told me. 'They don't see us, but we exist. It has to be this way until the crazies in the government reverse that fucking law.'

21 October 2013, on his birthday, he founded the club by hosting a small party of fifteen persons (all gay) in his small off-campus flat that he was still retaining. He named it Party BomBoy (PBB).

This party brought to 11 the number of PBB events I had attended. From concerts, open mikes, readings, exhibitions and emporiums, retreats and picnics to poetry slams.

The DJ scratched the groove and it seemed the roof would come down on us. Highlife is energy. My dancing partner at the moment was Maima, a writer from Lokoja. We rocked on. Two prisoners just let loose. Energy.

It was that time in every party, that time when it turns into a whirlwind. Booze and afro-beat-enhanced ecstasy. That time when you lose your partner to the crowd, and indifferent to the loss because you are absorbed in rocking with someone else. Everybody becomes generous with his partner, his spirit, his smells and his sweat.

C Boy and I left the party to chat a bit before re-joining. Two months before, I had told him that I was writing about the gay movement in Northern Nigeria and needed an interview with him. So, since we were both so overscheduled, we had pre-arranged a brief interview for this night.

We sat by the doorway, on the seats by the check-in desk. We talked, sharing cigarettes and drinks. Today, he appeared fatigued and slimmed-down. His eye bags sagged in an unsettling way. 'I am just battling depression but trust me always, your nigga is fine,' he said when I tried to find out what was wrong. We laughed; pecked each other. I asked for his permission to record our interview and he sipped his drink, smacked and nodded. 'You are asking that? Come on dude; don't make this nigga feel like a celeb. Come on.'

When C Boy founded PBB he never knew the extent to which the club would play important roles in the lives of young men and women like him. He had only thought of using the money he made from designing games and websites to support and house seven to ten people who were displaced because of their sexual orientation in his small flat in Zaria. He was shocked by the reality that surfaced soon after the club was founded. In less than a year, about 20 people showed interest and joined the club. Most of them were scared to come out to family and friends; others had been disowned and driven from home, homeless, needy and hungry. C Boy was in a fix: money, meeting tuitions and housing costs were huge challenges.

I asked how he coped with the situation. He lit a cigarette and thought for a moment before starting to respond.

'Man, it was fucking tough. You know, starting a group, a movement like this one is not like running a political party. It's not a project anyone, including the NGOs here, wants to support. How can you register a group that is already criminalised and demonised even before its emergence? Man, it was fucking tough.' He stopped speaking for another drag, tapped the ash on the ashtray and continued. 'The solace was only in the reality that I could bring troubled people together so they could share their problem in a close but warm space. Survival was a challenge but, you know, just as they say, a problem shared is half-solved.'

Early in 2014, PBB was able to pay for two flats in Kaduna and Zaria respectively, for any homeless and troubled member to live in. Both were equipped with studies, computers and Wi-Fi. PBB was able to pay tuition for 23 students of its 'parentless' and homeless members in different colleges and universities across Nigeria, and also provide living stipends from all these sources.

Though the main funding for PBB came from C Boy, the club was able to diversify its sources of funds. Having paid to train some members in photography, filmmaking, fashion design and App creation, the burden of funding lessened. Almost everyone was a freelancer of some kind. More funds came from ticket sales for open mikes, poetry slams, exhibitions and concerts. 'These events are the major strategies through which PBB sends coded signs to society that homosexuals exist here, and are ready to continue existing regardless of any law against them,' C Boy told me. Most of the artistic outdoor events in Kaduna, Zaria, Kaduna, Jos and Gombe were hosted and managed by PBB's team of concept developers. And of course, strict measures were laid down and followed to keep secret the identities behind the events. 'We are making society feel our energy by curating these events.'

C Boy chuckled and shook his head when I asked why he wasn't allowing PBB to reach out to foreign organisations sympathetic to the cause of LGBT. 'I don't believe in that bullshit,' he began, rubbing his eyes. He stood up and scurried to the DJ booth, spoke into the ears of the DJ and returned immediately.

'So sorry for that. Just reminded him to allow time for our brainstorming session. It's important.'

He sat facing me, his back to the dance floor. I looked across his shoulders into the crowd to see if I could find my partner. I didn't see her. It seemed like everyone had found the space and time to dance for the first time in their lives. The music blared, the groove continued.

I lit another cigarette. C Boy stared at me with those bored eyes. I reminded him of the question I had asked; he rubbed his eyes again.

He didn't like the idea of foreign aid to Africa in whatever form or guise, particularly 'using Africa as a sympathy tool to benefit from an organised system called "corporate responsibility"'.

'You see, it's so easy to attract sympathy for this kind of cause. Internet and all that, you know,' he said, snapping his finger to show how easy and fast it is to let the world know. 'But the issue is this, we, these guys here, all of us, don't want to be used as ad contents and objects. I don't want any social media sympathy-campaigns, especially those inspired and promoted towards Western organisations. Doing that would be objectifying our dreams, our passions and our bodies. It would be like organised prostitution. It's cheap, and fucking cruel to what we are trying to do.'

'We are learning to stop looking up there (the West) by working out how we can help ourselves here. How long are we going to keep asking for aid and foreign assistance?' He stopped talking, and reached for his wine.

C Boy told me about his guests – stories defying mainstream narratives about LGBT people in repressive societies like Africa. Stories of pride, ambition and rebellion. There was Musa (not his real name), 23, an Igala Muslim on the dance floor, whose widowed illiterate mother accepted his sexuality; he worked as a studio engineer to support his family. There was Kenny, 27, a graffiti artist who's a born-again gay Christian who left home two years before in search of love. He was hoping for things to improve for gays in Nigeria so he could marry in a church. C Boy showed me a girl, 22, in a jacket and mini-skirt and heels who was studying Biochemistry and working on a book on Women, Islam and Sexuality in Northern Nigeria. She was yet to let any family member know her sexuality. Sitting round a table with friends was Joshua, a married 45-year-old man and a lecturer in a polytechnic. He was the oldest man in the club. C Boy told me Joshua was preparing a divorce, and hoped to leave the country afterwards. He seemed to be the only one there seeking a new place.

Everyone here recognised the legitimacy of his sexuality. 'We'll be happy knowing this until death comes', C Boy said in conclusion. 'And we're glad we know this. Our feelings are legitimate. Fuck whoever thinks otherwise.'

He sipped his drink, heaved the sigh of someone with a lot of things to say, facing huge difficulties saying it.

He lit a cigarette. Instead of smoking it, he held it between his fingers and stared at the cigarette glowing and slowly shortening.

Depression is so disrespectful, so harassing.

I once confided in a boy when I was at university about my battle with depression since childhood and he gave me this are-you-fucking-serious look. 'Africans don't suffer from depression,' he said. 'It's one of those fashionable things black men say now to sound sophisticated like the white man, like being gay,' he continued, to further undermine the genuineness of my feeling. His opinion broke me down for two reasons. One, the flimsy way humans treat each other. Two, he was a final-year student in Social Science. How could he be so stupid?

11:43 am. 11 March 2015, my phone beeped with this text: 'It's here today again. Like never before. Fucking me up like never before. I lost, lost today. Cowardly disappointing. That's me. Sorry!'

It was from C Boy.

The door was locked from the inside. We broke in. He was nowhere in the room. The windows were flung open. And when we reached the window by his bed and looked down, we saw him. He lay in coagulated blood on the concrete floor at the backyard. For all these hours he lay there dead with his split-up head, and none of his neighbours knew. He lay there and nobody knew. Death is a solo business anyway. Like depression, it is always a solo transaction. Always.

We called the ambulance. And when we reached his family, they pleaded with us not to reveal to anyone the manner of his death. 'I'm an elder in the church, please protect our name,' his father said on the phone.

The clothes on his bed, floor and chairs seemed like he had contemplated what to put on before climbing that window and diving off. There were half-closed books on his bed and table, and pencils, dictionaries, notepads, papers, a teacup, ashtray, spoons, erasers, pencil sharpeners, spiral-bound manuscripts, wrapped weed, a Bible, devotional books, unfinished cards of paracetamols and aspirin, bangles, and an HP laptop. He had been working on a book, a collection of essays reflecting on Africa's future. 'Dude, this book will shake this continent to its root. Fucking draggy, but I'm called to write this shit. You know;

good books always drag,' he said with enthusiasm one night in his flat.
He had just returned from seeing his family in Adamawa.

From where I stood in the room I could see a paper pasted on the wall.
I walked closer to read the words on it. It read AFRICA'S FUTURE
HAS NO SPACE FOR FUCKING STUPID BLACK MEN.

He signed the statement with his name.

After two weeks in the mortuary, the burial was eventually held on
a hot afternoon in Zaria. His siblings and his father didn't show up.

About 3 am. A dance contest and spoken-word/rap battle were underway. C Boy suggested we finally re-join the party. I paused the recording. We moved to the dance floor. And for first time since we came, I saw my partner, in a sweat, on the dance floor, trouncing her challenger.

We are the contestants. In us, Africa finds its true rhythm to contest.

If you stepped in here, you would see all of us – gays, lesbians, bisexuals: oppressed people – refusing to mourn the anti-gay laws. We are making a mockery of it; mourning, for us, is not a virtue. We are reinforcing our passion and existence in this hall, right now, in our own way. Unknown to the world, we are buzzing in here with energy and stamina and dreams. We are laughs. We are smart laughing fires. Our feet are fires; so are our waists, our tongues, our eyes and our passions. You would see us blazing, emitting prophecies. We are fires: smoky hot fires, ready to choke to death the places and imaginations that threaten our survival.

If you were in this hall, you would feel how we assert ourselves through music, words, dance, hair, fashion, technology, ideas and spirits. We are spirits. If you were here, you would notice that we are not the demons roaming your cities and villages with evil and sin in our bosoms. We are not wayward, perverse, queer, or funny lovers. We are children of our parents, children of this continent, children of nature, of imagination and of hunger. If you were in this club seeing the tears roll down our eyes, feeling the sweat on our bodies, pouring down our torsos to our pants, as we move to Afro-beat, Afro-pop, Highlife and

Juju, you would realise that WE ARE CHILDREN OF OUR GODS. We exist.

We are buddies, roomies, comrades; breaking loose from our chains and jumping off the ships sailing to places where our dreams and our existence would be lynched. We are the holy spirits, and we prefer battling and drowning in fierce oceans and keep safe our prophecies than to be lynched by foolish black men.

We are children of Africa. And we care to be so.

The contests were concluded. We took a break for tea, for cigarettes, for booze, for toilets: for transition. We are the most prominent feature of Africa's transitioning; in us Africa truly rises. Girls headed to the restroom carrying handbags, toothbrushes and pullovers. The men seemed not to care; they loitered around, chatting, wineglasses and teacups in hand, wiping off sweat from their bodies, smoking. I grabbed my partner's camera; I snapped anything and anyone I could see. Bottles, shoes, cigarette packs strewn all over the floor; silhouettes of couples smooching around the corners; guys mixing drinks at the bar and yelling at each other; the afro or dyed or locked or Mohawk or plain hairdos, I snapped them all, the girls returning from the restroom and the boys rearranging the seats. I snapped them. Here, we are the photographs of Africa's budding *pluralities*.

And when we settled down to begin the brainstorming session we all smelled of sweat, booze, cigarettes, confidence and excitement. This is the best part of every party, the time when you don't complain of your neighbour's smell because it's a familiar smell, because it mingles with your own. Smells of mutual experience and lust.

Switching from party mode to intellectual discourse was a drag. Everyone whispered and yawned and chewed and belched: the hangovers from partying. The seats had been rearranged in a circle so we faced one another no matter where we sat. I ran my eyes through to figure our number. We were 41. 17 girls.

C Boy and Jenny, the tallest girl and person in the party respectively, launched the session with impassioned speeches.

I continued recording. We were talking about Afro-modernism.

Insights. Theories and counter-theories. Quotations and misquotations, and their debunking and deconstructions. Insults. Anger. Fierceness. Applause. Table banging. Wisdom. Foolishness. Completedness. Unfinishedness. Smelling mouths. Tongues of fires. Energy!

Africa is enlarging itself to become a CENTRE too. Africa is coming out to make visible its own CENTRES, headquarters, laboratories and metropolises. Africa is rising. Rising from the centuries-old folly of stupid black people. Africa is de-scribing itself, re-scribing itself and pre-scribing its future; it is reinventing itself through the mouths and imaginations of its babes and sucklings. For out of the mouths of babes and sucklings shall come forth mysteries and inventions and innovations and assertions.

We are babes and sucklings. And our tongues and imaginations are fires.

These are the various points and insights from the brainstorming session.

We are neither a theory nor a movement. We are open-space: Africa's newest genre. We are the *unemployables*, dissidents, techies, pan-Africanists, designers etc. **coming out**, in the 21st century, in our different corners, to challenge the centuries-old notion that *Africa does little thinking, trades badly, and is even worse at buying.*

'Afro-Moderns do nothing but look at and in and with and for Africa and its future, with the hope of re-inventing and re-energising it,' BabanGida, 26, said. 'We are economists, industrialists and investors renegotiating Africa's trade terms and conditions. We are not "white-collars", aspirants or mere civil servants or lame creatives. Afro-modernism makes the case to stretch "all of this" continent to the space where it becomes the centre of the world.' He concludes his point to thunderous applause and yells.

Afro-Moderns are renegotiating and/or terminating the skewed contracts, contracts signed by our forefathers and their stupid descendants in power who are still ruining the continent today.

Afro-Moderns know how badly their stupid forefathers performed in the past and are now refusing to mourn it. They know about colonialism and slavery and neo-colonialism and imperialism and other isms unfavourable to Africa, but are not going to keep wailing over the deeds and greed of devilish, vile, horrendous and criminal white people like those idiotic *postcolonial* scholars did, the people who squandered a precious chance, before and after independence, to create a true continent. Afro-Moderns are neither Afro-Romantics nor Negritudes. They are not critics and insulters of white people, or the other kinds of crap.

Afro-Moderns are interested in a non-romantic view of Africa. That's how they hope to see it well, and thereby recreate it. That's how to create its new curricula, its new politics, its new arts and aesthetics, its new business, its new industry, its pluralities.

Afro-Moderns are men and women whose only family, industry and business is Africa. And the constant pursuit is to expand, diversify, energise, imagine and re-imagine it. We are farmers, engineers, artists, technocrats, industrialists, scientists, negotiators; professionals living and working for Africa with the sole aim of growing, raising and branding it. We are homosexuals, heterosexuals, bisexuals, transsexuals and whateversexuals burning to rescue this continent from the ruins of stupid black men. We are not only the turning point generation; we are also Africa's hugest turning, biggest point, and boldest generation.

Ishaku, 24, was on his feet describing what he preferred Afro-Modernism to be known as when one of the bouncers walked in to C Boy and whispered something in his ear. They left for the door together, talking in low tone.

It wasn't long. C Boy hurried back into the hall, to the DJ booth and pulled out a bag. He put something that I didn't see in his back pocket and walked back to the door. He looked troubled.

It was 4:15 am. Something was wrong. One by one, everyone

moved to the door.

We heard sirens blaring at a distance from the club, approaching. There was a push at the door. A scamper, as everyone ran back to the hall. No one seemed to know what it was exactly, but the word 'police' was on everyone's lips. 'They've come for us. We are busted,' someone, I don't remember who, said.

The sirens were outside. Someone gave C Boy a hard push from the door and he fell backward into the hall. He quickly stood back on his feet, as seven masked policemen, armed with guns, walked inside. There was a huge silence. Another officer, without a mask and gun, walked in after his men. The officers began searching the DJ booth, the restrooms, the bar and the dark corners here and there. It took 10–15 minutes.

They returned and, gun pointing, asked all of us to sit on the floor. We sat. Nobody dared to speak.

'Who's Marshal here? Marshal Dominic?' The officer asked no one in particular. There was no one. No Marshal here.

'No one here goes by that name.' It was Joshua speaking.

At this time, one of the policemen located a light switch to the brighter lights in the club and turned them on. The club/laser lights were too weak to see real faces. The officer had a photograph in his hand; he started moving from person to person, comparing their faces to the picture. He walked round and didn't find a match.

He came back to where he was, and nodded to the policemen to move to the door. It was tense. I felt a pain in my chest. Everyone stared at him with eyes that spoke of fear of lynching or imprisonment.

He looked at the photograph again before bringing his eyes to us, searching. Then he cleared his throat. 'This guy is a murderer and we got tipped he would be here this night. He clubs here.' He moved closer to us, raised the photograph for us to see. 'Anyone seen this guy?'

We shook our heads.

He walked out. They walked out. The sirens started again. And they left. Fear dehumanises. Fear of being caught as gay in Nigeria demeans one's humanity. Fear of Nigeria's police arresting you for being homosexual crushes every gut you have.

Jenny burst out crying. Joshua rushed to her, put his hand round her and started crying too. Leila joined in, Kenny was groaning, and my partner walked to me and let out a loud cry. Then everyone began crying as if we had just turned orphans.

Tears taste like salt. Our tears. We are salts. Africa's salt. And we are here shedding tears because we are trampled upon on every side. But these men don't know this: that the more they trample upon us, the tastier we become.

Musa stood up, started for the restroom. As he turned to the door, he fell down. A heavy crash. We rushed to him. He was having a fit, the fiercest convulsion I have seen all my life. His hands and legs shook turbulently, like they had a life of their own.

There was commotion. We ran back and forth, with water from the restroom. We pulled off our clothes and fanned him with them. I ran outside, and our friend with the car was there waiting. I ran back in, and we carried him into the car. Joshua and Kenny sat at the back and we laid him on their legs. My partner sat in front. They drove off to the hospital.

It was 5:13 am.

Everyone sat about in the hall, fatigued and broken. C Boy sat on the seat by the check-in.

I joined him. We sat in silence.

I lit a cigarette and gave it to him. He refused.

'Look at the boy, the poor boy. Did you see him?' He started talking, his voice nearing a cry. 'What had he done to be frightened in that way? For being something else?' I didn't answer.

'We may have ended this event on a bad note, but I tell you we've made a huge statement. We've started something.' He brought out a revolver from his back pocket and kept it on the table.

'I can't close my eyes and let anyone hurt any of these people. I can't. Dude, I can't.' We sat in silence. A few people started to leave the club.

'I need to leave,' I said. C Boy didn't respond. He stared down. I walked to the bar for water, and when I returned he was no longer sitting on the seat. He was on the floor, crying and asking, 'what have we done to be scared to death like that? What did that small boy do to deserve such a scare? What?'

I didn't answer. If I did, tears would start running from my eyes. So, I just stood and watched this 27-year-old man sitting on the floor and weeping because he was homosexual. I didn't answer.

Boy, that night was energy. The night I last saw C Boy.

Suicide is a means of taking flight to hibernate too, a means of kinetic energy too.

Fuck whoever thinks otherwise.

The shea prince

CHIKÉ FRANKIE EDOZIEN

IT'S TAKEN 12 HOURS ON A 'LUXURY' bus to get here. My noise cancellation headphones block the relentless gospel music the driver favours. I rock to my heathen divas – Tina, Mariah, Beyoncé – and look out the window, watching the Ghanaian landscape change from verdant to sparse.

My first impression of Tamale is that it's dry, dusty and low rise; not like overcrowded Accra. The Twi murmurings there are replaced here by smatterings of Hausa and Dagbani. I haven't crossed a border but I feel I am in a different country. I've journeyed up north in search of women. Those dynamic women who, after trudging for miles at dawn, picking up shea nuts, process them into butter by hand.

This butter is used in confectionary products, but is better known for properties that nourish hair and skin. It is now a key ingredient in the cosmetics trade. The women who pick shea have rarely had a chance to go to school, but the income from shea pays for their children to stay in school. One of those 'shea babies', now an adult, is helping me navigate the terrain.

His name is Will and he's a heartthrob. I've come to write a journalistic piece on economic development and my focus is now derailed. I'm distracted and 'Heartthrob Will' is the culprit. We converse about shea but veer off into other things. I'm not sure how old Will is, but he estimates he's 37. Like many Gonja people, he doesn't have a birth certificate. He was born in a hut near Navrongo and uses a national holiday here as a birthday, putting that down on forms and also celebrating himself on that day, like other people do.

Will has made sure his own children were born in a hospital, where births are customarily recorded. Today he's a clerk for a non-governmental organisation, with dreams of owning a coffeehouse. He's been married, divorced and married again. He remains a babe magnet. The women hover. It's easy to see why. He's skinny and very dark, but his smile and savvy fashion make him stand out among the other tall dark men in Tamale. He favours form-fitting Tees, jeans and sneakers in a place where traditional dress is often de rigueur. He has a full head of hair and delights in sporting Mohawks, with shaved-in lines. The goatee and a high watt smile emphasise his deep dimples. He oozes vitality in a laid back Tamale. I've found a dandy.

Will comes from a long line of shea processors. I am impressed by his deep knowledge. But it is his melodic way of stringing together common words in English, his particular form of elocution, that makes me smile even when he isn't saying anything profound. As I take notes, I feel I will not use him in my story. Instead, I find myself inviting him to join me and my friends for dinner at Mike's Place, a pizzeria with al fresco seating that is popular with the expatriate crowd.

While we eat he says little, but focuses on me intently, staring whenever I speak. I think we might be in flirtation territory. There is an undercurrent, a nice vibe that feels like 'we should be talking alone and not with your friends'. I get nervous and wonder why he isn't wearing a wedding ring. When he bids me farewell and says he'll be in touch, I'm not sure I'll hear from him at all. Maybe I should have invited him to eat with me alone.

However, Will calls the next afternoon, while I'm on the bus back to Accra.

He tells me – he doesn't ask but tells me – he'll be visiting me the following weekend.

You're not going to ride the bus 12 hours just to see me are you? I ask, somewhat incredulous.

Of course I am, he says.

* * *

Will reminds me of Lamido, my first love back in Nigeria. That Alhaji gave me my first taste of the brutal reality of losing at love to culturally appropriate choices. Will has converted to Christianity from Islam. The name William is what he has adopted but not what his family uses. I take to calling him his northern name, Anass. Our banter is easy. He has this way of punctuating his sentences with emphatic exclamations – *Perfect!* And *Yes please!*

While speaking on the bus ride back, he asks if I am married. When I say 'no' and add that I am gay, he moves on to other things. No surprise, no curiosity, no questions. As if I've just said, 'I don't like socks.' Often Ghanaians I meet will say they've never met any openly gay man or they have a cousin they aren't close to; or simply make a religious comment when this comes up. But Anass just keeps talking, without pause.

When he gets to Accra the next weekend he wants me to tell him more about Nigeria. He seems already to know plenty about my homeland and regales me with tales from the Nollywood movies he's seen. He often pronounces a variation of my Igbo name: *Chikenna!* On occasion he calls me *Omalicha*, or 'the beautiful one'. Anass has never left Ghana but such is Nigeria's soft power that Anass uses intimate Igbo phrases.

We speak in hushed tones, with wide eyes, and I think to myself: 'Are we toasting each other?' We may be. 'Toasting' is a Nigerian way of flirting with words.

In this spacious flat I'm renting, we spend a lot of time reclining on the king-size bed and Anass uses Nigerian Pidgin slang to describe his conquests.

I chop am well well oh. I just dey fire dey go!

On his belly are a series of long Gonja tribal scarification marks. I begin to refer to them as the 'wall clock'. There is a huge circular marking with 12 long slim tribal marks that seem to jut out from his navel, three to the north, three to the south, east and west. The marks are elaborate and I find them stunning. I often trace my finger over them.

These marks look like a work of art painted on his flat stomach canvas. When he has his clothes off, I can only stare. Anass's lean muscular physique silences me.

That first weekend he's with me, we spend a lot of time indoors, in bed. Chatting.

When he arrives, he calls the Mrs and says, after hanging up, *there are some things you must do as a husband.* He says the reason why some men aren't married is because they don't want the responsibility of taking care of a woman or having to check-in like he is doing.

Anass has this way of reasoning that is so old-school – but I can't bring myself to chastise him for being chauvinistic. For instance, he says to me that he no longer cooks because he's no longer single. *Why should I go to the kitchen when I'm married?* That is the wife's domain. Just like picking shea is women's work. Yet in my flat he joins me at work in the kitchen and cleans up afterwards.

Or there is the way he explains his penchant for chasing and fucking younger women: *I can't be with a girl my age or older. That's too old.* 'Too old for what?' I ask. And he responds simply 'to have children'. So I say, surely that can't be the sole reason for marriage? He laughs. He always laughs. With me and at me. It's contagious. We laugh at our disagreements.

Like me, he loves animals and has several cats and birds. I've grown up in the huge megacity that is Lagos, attended university in America and now I work professionally in journalism. I'd call myself worldly;

he calls me Western. He's grown up in a rural area near Navrongo where farming was his way of life until he completed high school. His worldliness today comes from pop culture. He loves Nigerian music and introduces me to new artists I haven't yet heard of. Yemi Alade's hit 'Johnny' becomes our favourite song to dance to at home. The ditty is about a lover looking for her man, a lothario juggling many women.

Anass comes down at weekends and I find myself more eager than usual for Fridays. He has been to Accra before, during his school years. But when he visits me, he's charmed by the city, or at least by the slice of it I inhabit. Every time we walk out of my flat, he smiles and runs his long black fingers over the big wooden butterflies outside. His old roommate drops by a few times but mostly Anass ties himself to my apron strings. We go 'dancing' at the Shisha Lounge, an upscale nightclub, on Saturday nights. We don't always dance but we soak up the ambience. We have nightcaps at Republic Bar & Grill, the lovely roadside chop bar. I down several 'akpeteshie' and hibiscus cocktails, known as the kokokroto, and I share my spicy roast chicken and fried yam chips with Anass, who is a teetotaller.

On Sunday morning we go to church, with friends. With these accomplished and moneyed professionals, he engages lightly but keeps his attention on me. Later, Anass will tell me how impressed he is with them. He is particularly fond of Andres, the American foreign correspondent who is a brother to me. When we go to Andres's Sunday Fun Day poolside gatherings, Anass chats briefly with the expatriate circle folk and then swims with me. Every restaurant I take for granted is a revelation for him: from the Senegalese French bistro, Au Grand Ecuyer to the Nigerian Thai sensation, Zion Thai, off Oxford Street. He smiles big, having a ball. Weekends with him remind me of the first time I went to London. I was awestruck by everything from the pavements to the underground Tube. Now I'm awestruck by Anass being awestruck at our outings in his own capital city. Anass is wide-eyed in Accra even though he's seen it before.

But not like this. With you everything is nicer, he says over milkshakes at Pinocchio, an Italian ice-creamery in Osu. Until this time, he has mainly had the wonderful cuisine from up north; rarely desiring anything different. The dish, Tuo Zaafi, popularly known as 'TZ,' and 'kontomire' soup, a spinach delight, have been sufficient. Sometimes, we chow down on a northern staple, guinea fowl roasted on an open fire. It is fun for me to enjoy these routine outings with someone who is close to my age but doesn't know how to drive. And is bowled over by Thai iced tea. Strolling at dusk is our favourite pastime.

My pals find Anass charming and assume we are dating, until he says something about his wife and kids. They are certain I wouldn't be dating a closeted man. I smile and whisper: *He's not gay. We're just hanging out.* My friends are mostly heterosexual but Anass is new territory for me. None of them talk to me in soft whispers, or look me intensely in the eye, or send me text messages telling me just how grateful they are for my existence. I never wonder if my friends are 'toasting' me. I have no desire for romantic moonlight walks with them either. None of them, when I'm out of town, wait for me to call and say I've arrived safely before they go to bed. Anass does and says: *I have to keep vigil until I know you are safe. Now I can go to sleep.* With Anass I feel special. I feel loved.

* * *

My brother-friend Kenneth says one day I'll have to accept Anass's invitation to stay at his home in Tamale, rather than at my preferred hotel. He says I'll have to be prepared when his wife pulls me aside and explains that she is aware of our relationship and happy to have a co-wife. I burst out laughing hysterically. *She will tell you she has a lot of work to do with the children so you will have to be on duty all weekend handling his dick so she can rest.* These jokes made me more confident. The next time we meet up and are luxuriating in my bed, I ask – does he not want us to sleep together? I want to. And I've wanted to from the very first handshake.

He seems nervous and then he says: *You know I have children. For us that's a taboo.*

I'm not sure who the 'us' is. His Christian community? Or the Gonja people perhaps? Or maybe he just means being Ghanaian in general. He says he knows it's not that way in America, where I spend a chunk of my year working, but he lives in Ghana and while Chikenna is free to be, Anass isn't.

I put myself in his shoes for a moment. Recently, Ghana has been embroiled in a nasty national discussion about gay rights. Newspapers sell more when they blare 'HOMOS' on the front pages. Talk radio's favourite topic is which alleged gay to demonise and how to respond to governments like that of the United Kingdom tying development aid to LGBT rights. Evangelical groups are dispatching emissaries to rural chiefs warning them about the 'ills' of gays. This is the charged climate I slip in and out of, but in which Anass lives all year. I try to empathise, and I'm also feeling superior. Looking at me as if to knock back the smug look I have on, he warns me not to assume that he hasn't been with a man before.

Wait what?

Who told you I haven't been with a man before?

I let that last statement hang in the air; then say perhaps it isn't a good idea for us to be so cuddly if we are simply friends. His mood is changing now and not in a good way.

But why, why, why! Do you want to break the relationship?

Anass insists that we are special in our own way and that's that. And when I get married he will be my 'Best Man'. Everyone gets married, even the gay guys in Ghana, just like in Nigeria, he says. And when the children come, after having ceremonies in Nigeria, we will do an outdooring, a public 'sip and see' with the baby, here in Ghana. Now my mood is changing. I'm howling with laughter.

Later, I wonder aloud to my gay friends in Accra, Peter and Kwabena. This couple say I'm being gullible. So often, they say, Ghanaian men are 'gay-for-pay'. But Anass asks for nothing. In fact, he often asks to share what he has with me. Perhaps the escape from the humdrum in Tamale to see me in Accra is enough for him. Maybe it's stories of places I have been and what they looked like that he craves. When we are home, he often asks to see pictures of places I've recently been to, like Lagos, New York, São Tomé and Johannesburg. Sure, I always pick up the tab at the bourgeois eateries we frequent, but he is constantly showering me with gifts too, especially the traditional clothes and scarves that I fancy.

One particular expensive gift he gives me is a fugu, a traditional woven top indigenous to Ghana's north. It is made of fine cotton, dyed and perfumed, and is much nicer than any of the ones I've purchased myself. I see the first flash of anger in Anass when, mistakenly, he thinks I've re-gifted that present to another friend. Some of my urbane Accra friends say to drop him. He's settled, they argue: wife, children and now he has an emotional boyfriend (me). They say, let him go get a real boyfriend if he has the gumption to.

But I don't. I justify it by saying openly gay men and straight married men can be close and I'm not going to overthink it. This is my lie. Anass isn't just a pal. There is a deep mutual attraction, one on which we both feel powerless to act. I love the unbridled joy that emanates from him when he sees me in public. The smile gets wider and he puts his arms around himself in a hug. Once inside, Anass looks deep into my eyes and tells me how much he appreciates me. I enjoy hearing him reiterate how special he finds me. And, as he smiles, his quivering blood-red lips come so close to mine and then just stop before we touch. Arousal and then confusion follow. But Anass never goes further. As we lie in bed, he brags about his past pussy conquests as I trace my fingers over the 'wall clock' on his belly.

* * *

When I return to America he 'WhatsApps' frequently. I'm dating and happy in my relationship, just as he is happily married. Everything's tidy. But I get upset when I miss his messages. I make an effort not to reach out too often but I do get his messages and respond.

After months, I return to Ghana. I have in my mind moved on. I head to Tamale. It is the rainy season. The moment I see him, the big smile appears. The moment no one is within earshot, he remarks how cute I am.

He shows me his new home: a house he is building that he says is 'ours'. When he insists we return to his current house because his wife has prepared my dinner, I think it will be weird. But any trepidation I feel disappears when dinner is served, with his wife, children and assorted relatives. I eat the TZ. I feel at home.

I return to Accra and at weekends he visits. Again he remarks how great I look. We talk about making love. Now he is insisting that our relationship couldn't ever be taboo. *When I tell my wife everything you do for me, she says 'he loves you'.* That night he tells me tales of divorced women who strut their stuff in Tamale. And of his friends who pursue them. The women are dubbed *BZs*, because they are *Bazan Wara* or women who are mothers but have left their husbands.

Somewhere between the story of the BZs and my nodding off, he puts his arms around me, gets serious and whispers: *You can never know how someone feels about you. I love you. Just because nothing has happened doesn't mean I don't love you. You don't know the future. Be patient.*

I turn to look at him and he looks me in the eye. He declares: *Chike, me and you, na – forever oh.*

He's whispering, this time with an intensity, to make sure I get it. Eyes wide open, eyebrows arched and no smiles, he turns my face to his and repeats.

Chike. Me and you, na – forever.

The man at the bridge

KIPROP KIMUTAI

JUST AFTER RIAKU BRIDGE, A PLACE where trees congregated at night, Kwambai saw the glint in a man's eyes and stopped his car. Stepping out, he peered into the dark. It was late so most men had gone, leaving behind only the most determined. The man was leaning on the rails of the bridge, his hands tucked in his tight jeans as if he possessed the night. Kwambai walked up to him, close enough to smell his dusty jacket.

It was the man who kissed first. He was cold and rough, yet Kwambai felt as if he was being fed hot mercury. He became eager too, and grasped the man's shoulders, as his tongue swivelled down to the man's chin and neck. The man grabbed Kwambai by the waist and drew him in, pulling their bellies together. And Kwambai, in that most unholy moment, remembered Chela that morning. 'These days you have a belly! You don't fear getting fat like that?' Her face was absent then, just an opaque, oval shape.

Kwambai stepped back to look at the man's face. He resembled Bob

Marley – strong cheekbones, narrow chin, a long nose. Wind rustled and Kwambai moved closer, this time feeding on the man's liquid brown eyes. The man reached over and stroked his lips.

'You are a polite man. I love those ones like you. Take me to your house. I hold you well.'

Kwambai's hand twitched. The man smiled and looked aside. Kwambai followed his gaze. There was nothing to see. Just silhouettes of eucalyptus trees in the dark.

'What is your name?'

The man bent and took out a roll of marijuana from his socks. He placed it in his mouth, lit it and inhaled. Men at the bridge never said their names. They hardly even looked at each other. Everyone came here for a quick release. But Kwambai pressed on.

'Tell me please.'

'Do you feel like ngwai?'

Even before Kwambai could shake his head, the man placed the marijuana in his mouth. He tried to inhale but couldn't. The man laughed.

'You are not a person of ngwai.'

That irritated Kwambai. He sucked strongly now with his eyes closed. The smoke went straight to his lungs and he coughed until the world blurred. The man held him by the waist until he calmed down.

'Suck again, beautiful. But let it cool in your mouth first.'

Kwambai tried again, holding his breath as the man stroked his nipple.

'You can call me Franco. So, are we going to your place?'

Kwambai opened his mouth but no sound came out. The man leant in. There were lines on his face. His teeth were tiny and brown.

'Stop playing these games, beautiful. You mean you will leave me here alone? And with all this hunger? And the way I have loved you already?'

'Franco, give me your number please?'

'Now, you are asking for phone numbers surely and the way my phone never has charge! How will you find me?'

Nevertheless, he keyed in his number when Kwambai held up his phone.

'I am feeling cold now,' he said when finished. 'Especially now that you are just going to leave me standing here.'

Kwambai tried to kiss him, but he walked away.

* * *

When Kwambai drove into his compound and stepped out of his car, he felt as if he had dissolved. He had to touch himself to affirm he was still there. Even then his house, with its walls of rough stone, intimidated him with its glow. He walked through the foyer, which had a tall archway of coloured brick, and took off his shoes. Once inside the house, he went straight to the living room. His food was waiting on the dining room table – a bowl with two palm-sized lumps of brown ugali and another bowl with chepkarta stew on which pieces of teliat had been sprinkled. He walked to the fridge, which was in the kitchen on the right side of the room, and poured himself a glass of mursik.

That was when he heard someone breathe close by. He turned and saw Chela in a corner of the living room. She was dressed in an orange gown. It looked pasted on her like an extra layer of makeup.

'These days you just come in silently to the house, like a rat, like a thief.'

Kwambai walked to the table and sat down. The ugali was warm and soft. The chepkarta took him back to his childhood joys. Chela cooked well.

'I am just tired, Chela. There is too much work.'

'A person does not get tired of his people,' she said, as she sat opposite him on the table. She placed her arms on the table. The underside of her arms were much lighter. The left one had a slightly raised scar which he loved to touch at night as she slept, imagining how she burnt herself as a child, when she tried to bake a cake in her mother's kitchen without permission.

'One day I will just leave you this house.'

He looked up at her. She had bent her head and tilted it to the side.

'It won't be my work to wait for you each evening. Even me I should go out there and search for what I can call my own.'

He kept eating. The idea that this house was as uncomfortable to her as it was to him was overwhelming. She always seemed to possess it. The kitchen and the garden outside were her provinces.

'Let us just keep working hard, Chela. Life is not easy.'

He reached over to cup her hands. Her palms were rubbery. Made him feel like a boy.

'You can plant the roses tomorrow, Chela. I know you will love that.'

'You mind over the garden. I won't suffer anymore. Tomorrow won't find me here. Especially now that the children are with cūcū.'

He loved those children. Kimaiyo, who was already seven, would smile so hard to show his missing teeth, making Kwambai afraid that his skin would fail to reset when he stopped. Chebet was just three. Few of words. Going about the house saying 'baba, baba'.

'Maybe come upstairs we talk a bit?' Chela asked, as her eyes watered. 'I shall make some masala tea.'

He kept quiet for a long time, until she withdrew her hand from his hold. Her breathing turned loud.

'If there is someone else, Kwambai, just tell me,' she said, as she stood and folded her arms. Her cheeks were trembling. Her orange gown was no longer pasted to her skin. It had billowed and taken on a shape that was independent of her contours.

'Let us not start this fight again, Chela. It is too late at night.' She closed her eyes and clamped a hand on her forehead.

'Ngai, I have never seen a man like you. I don't even know what I am doing here in the first place.'

She lifted an edge of her dress to wipe her eyes. He turned and looked at his food. He had not started on the second ball of ugali. But he had cleared the teliat and mursik. He stood up and began to walk away.

'Let me go and sleep.'

'You scare me, Kwambai,' she said. 'You are one of those quiet men who wake up one day and kill their whole family. But you won't try that on with me.'

She clapped her hands in fury when he began to ascend the stairs.

'And wash your hands before you sleep. What kind of person are you? Will you enter bed just like that?'

He walked obediently to the sink and washed. That night in bed, he curled in a corner and thought of Franco's eyes. He thought about how Franco had pressed against him, how the rustle of the trees had urged them on.

* * *

He called Franco the next morning at ten. Chela had left 15 minutes before and he was all alone at the patio, which faced the garden, relishing the sunlight that played on his feet. His voice shook when the call went through.

'How is it, Franco?'

There was static at first, then a voice rippled through.

'I am well, beautiful.'

'I saw it well to greet you.'

For a moment, Kwambai was afraid the call would disconnect. For a moment, all the shrubs and flowers in the garden turned into a mishmash of green, red and yellow.

'That is good, man. It is good to greet one another. I also ask that you mind about me. This hustling life is hard.'

'I have a little work.'

'Which one now?'

'Small, small things for the garden.'

He gave him directions to his house. Two hours later, the gate bell rang. Kwambai opened and saw Franco. He was a bit hunched and his trousers were too big for him. He was wearing dusty safari boots and his eyes kept darting about like that of a person who had seen too much.

'It is good that you have come.'

Franco reared his head and smiled.

'No one can refuse work.'

They walked to the patio, where Kwambai served him litchi juice. Franco gulped it down and Kwambai had to serve him more.

'Are you enjoying yourself?'

'Si, you called me for work?'

He was no longer the man in tight jeans, leaning against the bridge rails in the dark. This Franco was a man whose mouth was tight and whose eyes looked far away – at something only he could see.

'This is where I stay.'

'You have a good place.'

'Let me show you around.'

They stepped into the garden and Kwambai felt as if he was on new land. The spread of purple hearts and baby sunroses fascinated. Even the crimson flower spikes, on the tips of the branches of the bottlebrush trees, seemed to sway more pleasantly as he walked next to Franco, who smelt of cigarettes. They stopped at a patch of collard greens, just behind an enormous mugumo tree. There, as Kwambai spoke on the kind of digging that needed to be done, Franco reached over and squeezed his balls. His words petered out when Franco knelt and unzipped his fly.

They dropped to the ground and began to writhe like earthworms as they took off each other's clothes. Kwambai clawed the air as if it was a mattress he could dig his fingers into when Franco entered him. Franco tore a vegetable out of the soil and squeezed it hard until it dripped green fluid, all the while breathing desperately like a dying cat. He would press Kwambai's face onto the soil, forcing him to smell sodden leaves, while lifting his bare leg high to bite. The pain was searing but Kwambai would ask for more and Franco would give generously. Later, when they were done, they lay on the bare earth, shielded by the long shadows of the mugumo tree and the high stems of the greens. Neither of them wanted to stand. They had sunk into a mundane world.

'I enjoy spending time with you,' said Franco.

'Where do you live, by the way?' asked Kwambai.

'In Gachororo. Just here.'

He pointed and Kwambai blew into his ears, before gently licking inside.

'Who taught you these things, beautiful? You are so good. I should have you in my bed every day.'

Kwambai didn't reply. He could feel bits of twigs and leaves on the wet soil pressing into his skin.

'What were you doing at the bridge?'

'I had just finished work at Pato's. And you know the way I was itching. I had to get someone. You know those itches man, when they come, they come. What will you do? So I went down there at the bridge but guys had already left. But I couldn't leave. I leave and go where with all that hunger? Then I saw you driving. I knew, from your speed, that you too were hungry and looking. You make me so hungry, beautiful.'

Franco pressed himself against Kwambai and began to nibble his neck. Kwambai looked past the collard leaves and the lawn, to the edges of the house that could be seen. He closed his eyes and returned Franco's kiss. They went for a second round.

* * *

'Are you happy, Chela?' Kwambai asked.

They were sitting in the living room, where he was pretending to read a newspaper. Chela had just walked in from the kitchen, where she had been busy cutting and washing.

'What are you saying, Kwambai?'

'Wuot!' he said as he threw his hands up. 'We even call each other by our names. Where did sweetheart disappear to? Is there anything here really?'

Chela's eyes narrowed, as she stood before him and placed her feet so close together that she seemed about to topple. Kwambai licked his lips. He had laid down in the garden with Franco. He had smelt the earth. He couldn't wish it away.

'Is that where we have now reached?' she asked. 'I need to finish cooking. I was making your favourite – peas with fried sausages.'

Kwambai looked at the coffee table in front of him. It had been wiped clean. But somehow red stains were visible through its glossy veneer.

When he looked up at her, she was smiling.

'Talk to me, sweetie. Don't keep quiet that way. This is your house.'

She moved to the other side of the couch and began kneading his shoulders. It was tempting to lean back and let those skilled hands soften his tense muscles. But he smelt her hairspray and his eyes watered.

When he saw an ant crawl across the table, he sprang up.

'I am tired of all these – this – this – this – I never wanted all these things Chela.'

He picked up his glass of water and hurled it at the wall. It broke into shards and the pieces flew across the room. Chela kept still, her hands around her neck. Then, without warning, she let out a long, painful wail.

'Don't kill me, Kwambai. Woooiiii! I have children jameni. Have mercy on me. Woooiiii!'

He tried to reach for her, but she staggered back. She tripped on one of the sofa legs and fell to the floor. There, she screamed again and the air turned thick with panic.

The security guard from the adjacent house called out and knocked desperately on the door. When Kwambai opened, the man inquired as to what was going on. 'You know no one ever hears any sound from this place,' he said, 'so when I heard Mama screaming, I had to jump over the fence.' But before Kwambai could even answer, Chela appeared at the door and pulled him inside.

'Omondi, I cannot stay here anymore. This one has scared me today. Even with all this wealth, I can go. After all, it is not like I was starving before I came here.'

'Calm down Mama, calm down,' the guard kept saying.

'Look, Omondi. Look at that the broken glass. I won't stay here and wait to be killed.'

Kwambai snorted and held his hands up.

'You are overreacting.'

Chela didn't listen. She ran through the narrow corridor and up the stairs to their bedroom. Kwambai and the guard were left giving each other awkward stares. She appeared less than ten minutes later, dragging two heavy suitcases, tears streaming down her face.

'Now you will know what a home is like without a woman. You will understand how cold this house can be.'

She moved closer to Kwambai. Her yellow top was already sweat-drenched.

'I have done work for you for real. This house stands because of my back. Children I have given you. But when they are done staying with cūcū, they are not stepping inside this house.'

'Did you plan this all along, Chela?'

'Plan what? Do you think you are the kind of person who can ask me how to plan?'

Kwambai wanted to answer but felt Omondi's hand squeeze his shoulder.

'These things,' said Omondi. 'Just talk about them slowly. Let me go back to work.'

Chela grabbed Omondi's hand.

'In fact, you are the one to help me carry this luggage to the car.'

Omondi heaved a suitcase onto his back, took another one in his hand and followed Chela out of the house.

Kwambai stood still and listened to the crunch on the gravel as the Mercedes drove out of the gate. He kept standing until Omondi peeped through the door and said, 'Everything is okay now mzee. I will close the gate.'

He kept standing until evening came and the living room turned dark. That was when he lay on the sofa and slept.

When he paid Franco to move in two days later, Kwambai drew all the curtains in the house. They didn't leave the house except to collect deliveries of Hawaiian pizza and chicken burgers at the gate. Well-fed, they fucked until they were raw.

Kwambai would go to the toilet and be surprised that he was not bleeding, then go back to bed to find Franco eager again, his eyes enlarged as he streamed *Next Door Ebony* on a laptop. When satiated, Franco would walk around the house in his boxers, touching the walls as though they were about to vanish. On the third day, the house began to stink and it became impossible not to yearn for freshly ironed laundry and clean bed sheets.

'I need to make this house alive,' said Kwambai. 'There is too much shadow.'

They were on the sofa, Franco resting his head on his lap, his uncombed hair too rough to stroke.

'Are you worried, beautiful?' he asked, sitting up straight. He had a way of looking at Kwambai. A mixture of mockery and affection.

Kwambai felt his shoulders relax. He looked at the china figurines above the fireplace – a whale, a ballerina and a soldier. Chela had bought them from a roadside hawker when they were on honeymoon in Thailand.

'This woman will make you grow old so quick,' said Franco. 'And you know you have not paid me for my gardening?'

He stood before Kwambai, his skin looking as smooth as soft clay. 'You will also have to pay me for the work I did today.'

He held his arms akimbo. His belly protruded a bit, but his shoulders were fine, with strong muscles shaped like buns. Kwambai reached for his wallet in his back pocket and took out a thousand-shilling note. He held the note's edge and it waved in the air. Franco snatched it and leapt back on the sofa, to lay his head on Kwambai's lap once more.

'Enjoy me while I am here. You married men are complicated. You don't know how to relax and enjoy. And the way you love banana. My big, black banana.'

He began stroking himself.

'Maybe this is all I have ever wanted,' said Kwambai. 'I don't want this to end.'

Franco stood up and laughed.

'You married men just want everything to be yours. You want everything to carry your name. Even these walls. Even my flesh.'

Kwambai stood and kissed him. In the dark, Franco's lips were fuller, with a hint of red where they joined. Kwambai tried to part them with his tongue but Franco pushed him back.

'We need to clean this house. It is filled with rubbish.'

Franco opened the curtains to the living room. Sunlight streamed in and Kwambai, feeling exposed, hid behind the sofa. Franco, on the other hand, sat on the window ledge. He was a man who loved his body, who seemed at peace with the light that played on muscled arms. He turned to look at his lover. 'If you want me to stay in this house longer, you will have to clean it. And you will have to add my pay. This body is not built with wood.'

'Sawa, let us start by washing the utensils basi.'

In the kitchen, Kwambai realised the joy it was to dip his fingers in sudsy water. How easy it was to giggle when Franco touched his waist with cold fingertips. How easy it was to turn and take off what was necessary, so that their bodies could join and shut out the world. They made love all over the house, till they finally settled on a favourite spot, a tiny guest bathroom. There, Franco seemed smaller. Just a man who smiled shyly when Kwambai lifted his chin with a finger.

'How long will you keep me here?' he asked.

'I love you,' was all Kwambai could say.

* * *

It was the next Saturday that Kwambai saw his wife's Mercedes drive in. He kissed Franco on the forehead and told him to go and wait upstairs. When he opened the door, it was his mother Grace who walked in. Grace was dressed in white pants and a jersey with tropical prints, both of which had been bought by Chela on a trip to London. She walked slowly to the sofa and sat down. Her eyes had sagged since they last met. 'Chamgei lekwenyu.'

He greeted her back and smiled more than it was necessary.

'I hear she ran away, lekwenyu?'

'Who?'

'Your wife. She called me. She said that you were very angry.'

'There are things Mama. Things about me, which I believe you should know.'

Grace reclined on the sofa like a woman who had nothing more to offer to life but sagacity.

'I know, Kwambai. I know who you are. I saw you before you saw yourself.'

Her eyes lingered over him until her pupils began to dissolve.

'But you are my son. You must do what is right so that you can live in this land. You must do what is necessary, so that when you are old, you have your people. Those two children she has taken to her people are your children. At such times, you have to look at everything and decide whether life has to be like this. Look at this house. It stinks.'

More light came into the room. Clouds had shifted and released the sun. He had done his best to clean the house. But now, even the table seemed oddly askance. Each dark corner threatened to reveal hints of his sweat, his cum, his shit.

'You are my only son, Kwambai. I need you to carry your father's bloodline. I am just a vessel and so is Chela. We are here in this world to lean against our men and to give them children. That is why our people say respect is holy, it resembles a man. You are a man, Kwambai.'

Kwambai fiddled his fingers. He remembered the smoothness of his Italian tuxedo at his wedding. He remembered how he shook when the priest opened the Bible and asked him to swear on it. He remembered other things; how as a child he had walked inside a forest and wandered for long, until he found a stream of cool water to drink; how he sat by that stream all day until it was dark.

'I have told Chela to wait for me in the car, lekwenyu. You decide if she should come in or if she should go back to her people.'

Kwambai pressed the nail on his left finger until it turned pink. He thought of mursik and teliat, how they would melt in the mouth when combined with ugali and chepkarta. He thought of those hot evenings when they would leave the windows open and Chela would sit at the dining table as he scrolled through WhatsApp. He thought how easy it would be, to drive to the bridge each Friday evening, and stop for just 20 minutes.

Site visits

WELCOME LISHIVHA

ERNEST AND I HAD JUST STEPPED OUTSIDE Liquid Blue, the gay bar on 7th Avenue. We were tipsy and trying to get a cab to go home. Cab drivers were yelling around to people as they stepped out of the bar, 'Cab to go home! Cab to go home!' One cab driver, wearing a brown leather flat cap and a black leather jacket, approached us and offered to take us home at a discount. Instead of R80, he would take us home for R50. We looked at each other and agreed silently. Ernest sat in the front seat and I hopped in the back. A few minutes into the ride, I noticed that he missed the Enoch Sontonga Avenue exit.

'Where are we going? You were supposed to take the exit on Enoch Sontonga Avenue. We did say we are going to Braamfontein centre you know,' I said, half nervous, half bitchy.

'Relax I want to get beer,' he said, looking at me through the rear mirror and flapping his arm in the air. He stopped further down on Solomon Street after missing the Enoch Sontonga Avenue turn. It was dark and the only light around that area was coming from the street lights, yet there were people milling around, smoking. The beggars on the side of the street were still up, covering themselves with boxes and blankets.

'What is this? Where are you taking us? Why would you stop in the middle of nowhere?' I was suddenly wide-eyed and fearful. He stopped the car, then looked at me wordlessly through the rearview mirror. He asked Ernest to go inside the shebeen to buy him beer, leaning out his window, with a R20 note in his hand and pointing at what looked like a closed door. Next to the door, three men stood smoking. Terrified by the thought of being separated from me in the middle of nowhere, Ernest nervously let out a 'no way'.

The driver looked at us through the rearview mirror as if to check whether the coast was clear. Then he got out, leaving us alone in the car. He came back five minutes later with two Black Label Quarts. He started the car and we were driving again. Ernest turned back, looking at my face searchingly. I decided to break the tension and silence with conversation.

'We didn't even get your name earlier,' I said, feigning enthusiasm.

'Jabu,' he said, letting out a chuckle that I thought was directed at my poor attempt to probe without seeming to.

'And where are you from, Jabu?' I carried on, suspecting I might already be treading down the annoyance avenue.

'I live in town,' he said, pausing to open the Black Label with his teeth, 'You have a nice big ass,' he added and gulped the beer.

'And how long have you been in living in town?' I persisted, ignoring his comment.

'I live with my wife and two children. I've been there for ...' – he takes another a gulp and puts the beer in between his thighs – 'I've been there for three years now. I was in jail for about five years before I moved to Marshalltown'.

'But don't worry, I am not that dangerous,' he says, looking at me in the rearview mirror, sliding his hand from the back to caress my thigh, his eyes focused between the rearview mirror and the road. I politely push his hand back and say, 'I am okay thanks' – scared that asserting myself further might be lethal. I want to beat myself hard for not having been more careful in choosing our cab. R50 is too good to be true, we should've known better, I lament in my head.

'Why are you acting all fresh,' – he says lighting up a cigarette – 'as though you don't want it.'

Neither of us respond.

'I am always picking up boys like you in Melville and they're always keen. I don't know why you guys are being like this. Look at how fresh you are. You mean to tell me I'm losing out on this fresh meat?' he says as he rolls down the window, kind enough to blow the smoke out.

Neither of us respond. We drive for some time in silence while he smokes.

'Okay then. Let's go have some fun at The Factory,' he says throwing out the cigarette butt out the window.

He is now driving over Mandela Bridge towards Braamfontein centre. We calm down a bit as he heads towards our neighbourhood and we realise he's taking us home. But still, we don't respond. He pulls up outside our house and turns off the car. It looks like we are off the hook. He is not quite ready to let go, though. He gives it one last try.

'Okay then, fine. I'll pay for your entrance,' he says.

Until this point, I have never met anyone who has admitted to having been to The Factory. It always existed as a mythical place, with everyone having their own versions of what happened there. It was mainly known as a place where married men went to have sex with boys. This was home to male-only orgies with naked men everywhere. Almost every time The Factory came up, it was always spoken about as a place that 'apparently exists'. No one dared admit that they'd been, let alone laying an invite on the table.

Jabu begins to talk about The Factory and how often he goes. He is happy to share, hopeful that with each detail we might take up his offer. When he doesn't find a boy to sleep with, he goes there for a quick fix. We decline politely and he makes it clear he is heading there now because we have turned him down. Sometimes he takes boys there to go have sex with when he can't take them home because of the wife and children.

I spend the following few days coming up with my own versions of what goes on at The Factory. I am studying Anthropology at the University of the Witwatersrand and in need of a case for an ethnographic study where 'participant observation' was to be the research method. Participant observation is a mode of social inquiry that requires the investigator to be as immersed in the lived experience of the inquiry as the subjects of the study. That, in addition to my curiosity about the ways in which sex has been the central tool to the policing of queer people, was how I decided to explore and make sense of The Factory. So naturally, I headed out on my first site visit.

* * *

The Factory is an exclusively male nude bar located in Doornfontein, Johannesburg. It is advertised as the ultimate playground for men who want to leave their clothes and inhibitions at the door to indulge in their fantasies. From my experience, I found it to be predominantly a space that serves as an outlet for heterosexual-identifying men to seek sex outside the heteronormative order.

I spent a few days at The Factory in Doornfontein. In that time I wondered about whether it was a queer space – whether what went on there was a function of heteronormativity, a release from it or a space that challenged heteronormativity as an institution. I became increasingly curious about whether and how it might be possible to find a place for The Factory and other similar places that exist across the continent – within the paradigm of queer culture and politics. In providing this detailed account of the connections and interactions at work in this exclusively male nude bar I want to explore whether The Factory can be viewed through the lens of queer culture as a politically progressive space that transgresses the hetero-norm.

To do this, I want to examine The Factory through the lens of Counter Publics as outlined by Michael Warner and Lauren Berlant. In their paper, 'Sex in public', they posit that the privatisation of sex is where the policing of sex and morality begin. The idea that sex is an act that can only be accessed by a heteronormative couple in the bedroom has resulted in a public arrangement that is produced in every aspect of our social life. They posit that a range of assumptions about what happens in the privacy of the bedroom are made – and they permeate the public domain.

Warner and Berlant suggest that the best way to dismantle this kind of arrangement is through the development of Counter Public spaces that allow for queer people to enjoy sex while challenging the idea of sex being a private act that can only be enjoyed within the heteronormative institution. These spaces exist and ought to exist outside hegemonic practices of sex and sexuality and thus seek to challenge heteronormativity as the ideal sexuality. They create what Warner and Berlant call 'new forms of gendered or sexual citizenship'.

In his book, *The Trouble with Normal*, Michael Warner has argued that the moral high ground that is assumed in our predominantly heteronormative world is occupied by individuals or social groups that police the sexual choices, practices and lives of others. Warner argues that sexual shame and repression are dominant in a heteronormative society. He suggests that shame and sexual repression are crucial political tools used to determine who is included and who is excluded in a society. To transcend shame and repression, Warner posits that sex and sexuality must be viewed as political acts. I will use this idea of a Counter Public within the queer paradigm to understand how The Factory challenges or reinforces our understanding of sexuality.

* * *

My first visit is on a Wednesday afternoon. Because it was my first time, I thought I'd go on a weekday and at around 1 pm, when there would be fewer people. This would ease me into the escapade and not overwhelm the prude in me.

I embark on the long trip from Braamfontein to Doornfontein where The Factory is located. Walking there gives me a sense of how deserted and awfully quiet this area really is. I walk past Noord Taxi Rank which is almost always congested with traffic, pedestrians and street vendors. I walk past Ellis Park Stadium and China City Shopping Complex, wondering who on these busy roads might be coming from or going to The Factory. I am later told by one of the bartenders that some of the busiest nights are those when there are matches at Ellis Park.

The area is industrial; occupied by factories and abandoned lots. There are men in blue uniforms walking around, and seemingly workers on lunch break. It is extremely quiet. And there are about five cars parked outside. There is an old black man standing outside the entrance in a black security guard uniform. Above him is a sign saying, 'The Factory Bar'. I walk up to him and ask awkwardly, 'So … is it open?' He confirms that it is, displaying no discomfort himself. He points me to the door.

'Do you know if it's busy inside?' I ask as I head in the direction he has pointed.

'It's not that busy, Wednesdays at this time aren't usually hectic … but there are a few people inside. Go up those stairs, and ring the buzzer when you get there,' he adds.

I do as he says. The door buzzes like a doorbell – ding dong. I realise later that the sound creates a sense of anticipation for the people who are inside; they know to expect a new body. I enter a poorly lit area. Even on a Wednesday at 1 pm, the lack of lighting creates the illusion that it is night time. Soft ballad music plays in the background.

A young black man, seemingly in his late twenties, appears from the counter. He is completely naked, I peep to see his semi-erect penis as he approaches the counter.

'Sixty rands,' he says impersonally even though he looks as though he is assessing me. I take out R100 and hand it to him. He doesn't give me change. He explains that the balance is kept and each drink I order will be deducted from there. This makes sense because I will not have pockets for my wallet.

'So, are you having a busy day today?' I ask, trying to seem nonchalant.

'Not really. Take off all your clothes and hang them here. Leave your shoes on,' He says, handing me the hanger with a string marked '26'.

'Where do I change?' I ask as I grab the hanger.

He looks at me with what seems like annoyance.

'Right there,' he says walking away.

I think the number suggests that I am the 26th person of the day. Standing behind the counter, I start to take off my clothes. A young black man with a green string around his waist and an erect penis stands by and stares at me. I give him a blank look in turn, and then he turns and pretends to be reading something from the wall. I stop taking off my clothes to observe his brown skin glistening in the darkness of the room. He is reading a poster by Health4Men with pride colours across it that reads 'no one should ever be discriminated against based on race, religion' and in capital and bold letters 'AND SEXUALITY'. Health4Men is an initiative dedicated to eradicating and reducing the transmission of sexually transmitted diseases through research projects and ensuring access to HIV & AIDS resources. They provide The Factory with condoms, lubricant bottles and sachets.

Two other naked men stand next to the guy reading the poster. They stare at me while he continues pretending to be reading from the poster. I hand the bartender my clothes and walk through a small passage behind a counter. At the end of the counter is a right turn into the area. There are heaters and some walls are mirrored. The effect creates the illusion that the area is bigger than it seems. But it also serves as an interesting device for the body language that takes place. I glimpse people checking each other out through the mirror. Over the course of my visits, I will sometimes even see people admiring their own naked bodies and fondling their penises, looking at people through the mirror, as if to invite others to join in.

The place has a maze-like design, like an incomplete construction project. This is deliberate. It creates a feeling of mystery and intrigue; there is hardly an open space where everyone can see each other clearly, except for the bar area. Instead, it is full of corners, passages and little rooms with no doors. There's one room by the bar area – the only room that has a lockable door and the only room without a bed. It is the only room where you can close the door while having sex, masturbating or kissing someone. At the bar area where people can see each other, you'll find people standing around and watching porn on the television screens nearby. Sometimes people stand around as if they are waiting to see other people have sex – which, depending on the numbers, isn't that often. If something starts people generally flock to go watch; to masturbate as they watch.

In fact, hearing people have sex creates anticipation, builds up the sexual tension for and between the people watching. It is as if they are hoping to take turns, to join in. Occasionally two people making out or having sex loudly can get other people to also start making out too. There are three screens in the bar area constantly playing porn. At almost every instance the first screen displays porn with black men, the second shows only white men and the third screen shows interracial porn. The bartender DJs the porn by constantly changing the DVDs. There is no sound; the images are there to create an ambience and to distract people who might feel overwhelmed by what is happening in the area.

To display sexual interest, people will generally follow you around and attempt to caress you. All of this is done very gently and subtly. When making a move, it's almost as if there is a build up that starts with a nod or a wink, a gentle touch and then a reach to your genitals. A sign of discomfort or disapproval is enough to send anyone off. The place is also very quiet. The low sound level creates a safety net because if anyone tried making a move on you against your will, a scream or a raised voice would be heard by almost everyone in the bar.

There are 'glory holes' along the maze paths – apple-sized holes on the walls situated at an average height around the mid-section level, suitable for one to push a penis through to the other side for fellatio. There are also chains hanging by the bar area with handcuffs. During my visits, I did not see any sexual encounters taking place at either the glory holes or the chains.

The Factory has been running for 15 years this year. Rian van Wyk, who used to be a regular, says, 'The Factory has gone through several changes. It has moved from being a predominantly white bar to predominantly black and rather representative of the demographics of South Africa.' He said the first time he visited The Factory was on Valentine's Day when he was feeling 'sad, lonely and horny'.

It would be the first of many visits. That first time he was overwhelmed. As a result, he did not engage in a lot of sexual activities, he says. He often visited when he was feeling horny and wanted to, at the very least, be around naked men. 'My first few visits were spent trying to figure out the place and the activities that take place there,' he says. He started participating once he understood the signals, and the way everything worked. He says now he only visits occasionally because there are other spaces for gay men to meet. The Factory is mainly frequented by working-class black men. Although it is by no means a black-only space, black people represent the clear majority of patrons.

The only thing you are allowed to wear at The Factory are shoes, your watch and the string with your number. In other social spaces clothes are used as social markers, here the basis of judgement is the naked body. Of course, I could tell a lot about class based on the shoes and watches that the men walking around were wearing. There is a spot in the bar area where you can see people as they enter and pay the entrance fee before they take off their clothes. Around 1 pm, there are men who walk in wearing suits, ties and formal wear and often rings on their left ring fingers. These men have obviously left their workplaces for 'lunch'. Almost all of them leave after an hour. In discussions over my visits, I learn that they sometimes knock off early and pop into The Factory before going home to their wives and children.

I visit one Tuesday afternoon. It is not too full. There are about ten men inside. None of them are engaged in any sexual activities that involve physical contact. They are just walking around, looking at each other and watching porn on the screens by the bar area. Two men start kissing and fondling upstairs, in a narrow passage with a leather mattress that fades into darkness at the end. As soon as they start making out almost all the men in the bar gather around them – pleased to finally get some excitement. It doesn't take long before the small crowd disperses. However, there is something about the encounter that is too intimate to watch. There is no chance that this will become an orgy – no one else is invited. I walk away, surprised by how everyone knew to leave them alone – knew that they should not even be watching.

The Factory has a reputation as a sexually wild space. And yet what I have just witnessed is a moment of sensitivity and restraint. Over the course of my visits, I witness this repeatedly: respect of the intimacy of two people engaging in sex. In fact, most of the sexual encounters that take place at The Factory are very intimate in that they are about two people having a private encounter. I saw men holding each other and making conversation after a session of having sex, or simply holding hands and talking without any sexual contact.

Occasionally, like in the early hours on a Sunday morning, there would be a group encounter. This often involves several men taking turns to penetrate one person, often on the swing in the middle of the 'dark room'. Most 'participants' are passive – watching while masturbating.

Weekends are busier than weekdays. On weekends there are men everywhere. Some sit alone by the bar area, others walk around the bar, sitting in groups, around corners, chatting by the toilets. The dark room is at its busiest during the weekends. The dark room is one of the bigger rooms in The Factory, positioned at the end of the space – as though all the other hallways and passages lead to it. It is pitch black, so dark that I have to use my hands to navigate and ensure that I don't walk into a wall. I use my hands to check before moving forward until I find a spot on the wall where I can stand and watch. After my eyes adjusted, the only thing I could see were shadows; the outlines of people having sex on the bed right next to the tinted window. The people who have sex here know that their identity is withheld, their acts are anonymous.

In the dark room, there is something almost primal about the expression of desire. The idea of privacy becomes blurry. Sex is public and yet identity is not. There is always someone having sex, and there is often a gathering – a group of people watching the silhouettes. In the dark room, it's almost as if one is merely a body for sexual pleasure. Some people spot each other in less dark areas and once they have established interest, they head to the dark room and make out or have sex, where they can be heard but not seen. Or seen but not identified. Others find one another in there – and have sex so that their identities are completely withheld even to those with whom they are temporarily having sex with. One married man I speak to says he is only willing to have sex in the dark room, where he won't be seen by the person he is fucking.

One of the bartenders I speak to mentions that 'the notion of privacy remains extremely important to the clients'. Riaan, whom I quote above, agrees: 'The people in The Factory have a "no tell policy", a form of camaraderie so that if you see someone who goes to The Factory outside of The Factory, you keep quiet about it.' 'People look out for each other somehow,' he adds.

My site visits make me realise how important this distinction is. Some men – the ones who have sex in the open areas – sometimes simply want to have intimate sex without participating in any group activities. For them, The Factory provides a space to access intimate sex with men. Some of the men in the Dark Room are looking for a different sort of privacy. They need the sort of privacy required by people whose sexual lives must remain secret, particularly because they are engaging in an activity that doesn't conform to heteronormativity. For them, privacy is the price they pay for their subscription to the heteronormative order.

It is precisely because of this that The Factory serves as a limited

Counter Public. It provides an outlet to heterosexual-identifying men by creating a space in which sex is no longer limited to the bedroom of a heterosexual couple. But it achieves this in private ways that maintain heteronormativity as the sexuality presented as ideal in the public. It locates itself both within and outside the heteronormative framework. The majority of people who go there do so on the down low. It is important to them that they maintain their position within a heterosexual society.

It is men like Jabu – the cab driver who introduced me to The Factory – who stand to be the ultimate benefactors of The Factory. They can enjoy The Factory while preserving their heteronormative lives as fathers and husbands. Many of the men who go to The Factory are married, closeted gay men and generally heterosexual-identifying men. They are men who insist on keeping their experience of The Factory a secret for the sake of their reputations within the heteronormative order.

The very existence of The Factory, and what it has to offer, can only be celebrated within the context of the kind of privacy that is linked to the shame of not confirming to heteronormativity. In other words, the privacy practised at The Factory does not function to deepen intimacy alone. The privacy mainly exists because its patrons are ashamed of what they do there. Its patrons get to enjoy an escape from the societal pressure of constantly performing heteronormativity. Yet, this is done in ways that co-opt queer spaces as mere outlets of heteronormativity and not alternatives that subvert heteronormativity as the ideal sexuality. Although The Factory does not shake the foundation of heteronormativity, by providing an outlet for heterosexual identifying men to indulge in sex outside the hetero-norm, it does put pressure on heteronormativity – rendering cracks that demonstrate that the heterodoxy is impossible to sustain. What The Factory calls 'privacy' – but which is really a veil of shame – represents a form of moral panic. Yet there is scope for this shame to be transformed into a political tool of progress. Over time spaces like The Factory can and will help foster queer culture and the opportunity to create new economies of pleasure.

6 errant thoughts on being a refugee[17]

SARAH LUBALA

1

on the worst of my days
this body
is a gimcrack-vessel
no more than two lungs and
a tremor
nailed to salvaged wood

---

17 First published in *Brittle Paper*, 7 January 2017.

2

grief travelled with me
across the *Ubangi* River

i prayed love
and all her cognates
on the passage over:
libet (to please)
lips (to be needed)
lyp (to beg)

i arrived with
bruised knees
wet hair
a mouth-full of salted fish

3

i am so
hungry
hungry
hungry
for holiness
for communion
for a God you can sink
your teeth into

4

i was raised
on the Congolese-gospel
i can teach you how to forget
where you are from
to worship the wide road before you
hands open
like this:
make each palm
a letter
to the sky

5

Beni is a town
with one police station
airport
market
many graves

i should go back
my people are weeping

6

'home'
is a narrow bed to sleep in

Portrait of a girl at the border wall[18]

SARAH LUBALA

All the women in my life are hungry.

I have written this one hundred times
I do not know how else to tell it
how to write
the girl by the roadside
the bruised peach
the narrow collar
the night full of birds

Her body is a long river
that cuts through every room

---

18 First published in *The Missing Slate*, 23 February 2017

see her in the kitchen
see her standing behind the gate
see how she cups her hands
for soap
for bread
for sweet milk

Tell me
where do I put her?
this girl pressed against the border
this girl swallowing her papers whole
this girl bird-wailing through a fence

See her hands
holding the broken saucer
stitching the skirt's hem
cradling the last orange
begging the names of God

Where do I put her?
Tell me what is owed
here
the fist of hair
here
the cut lip
here
the legs
split like fruit

Who will take her?
this sorrow-of-home-girl
this river-of-bees-girl
this night-singing-girl
this throat full of ghosts

Notes on black death and elegy[19]

SARAH LUBALA

I

My father tried to kill his first wife
in a house with wide windows
and yellow hibiscus

II

My love does not know
I have never stood naked
before a man

---

19 First published in *The Missing Slate*, 23 March 2017.

III

For weeks I have tried to write an essay
on 'Black Death and Elegy'
I compose letters instead:
Maman,
I am writing to you from across the water
the years have been a heavy tide
against the shore of me

IV

So much sits on the throat
the men on roadsides
the men in corridors
my wrists are living birds
small and keening beside me

V

My uncle
gone some twenty years
telephones at dinner to tell me
he was once a child soldier

Oh Lord
the years kneel down

Human settlements

TSHEPISO MABULA

THE DICTIONARY DEFINITION FOR A HOME is 'a house, apartment, or other shelter that is the usual residence of a person, family, or household' but for many, the reality is that where you lay your head down is where you call home. Many residents of Johannesburg have travelled from far and wide to find greener pastures; they have made this vibrant city their home while they hustle to provide for their families who are left behind, hoping for a better life.

As the child of a working-class family from the rural Eastern Cape, I know all too well how it feels to have to recreate a home, far away from home. You find this foreign space, with cold, unfamiliar walls and you somehow need to turn it into your home. So you do that – you add items that represent you and remind you of the place you left behind, so that the one you are now in can feel just as warm and loving as the one you left. You add facets of yourself, personal belongings and eventually you get used to that space, it becomes your place of comfort, your serene sense of bliss, where you rest your tired body after a hard day's work.

For many people the city of Johannesburg is a place with no guarantees and it is a place of uncertainty; this uncertainty is evident in the recent building evictions in downtown Johannesburg, resulting in the displacement of many residents.

This essay looks at the relationships people create with the spaces they inhabit using the recent evictions of residents in Johannesburg buildings. The people who evict the residents are just doing their jobs, earning their keep. But in the process many people are left homeless and many of them are unable to return to their homelands because the reason they are in the city is to provide for the people back home.

This essay looks at how people from the same socio-economic spectrum were pitted against each other in a single day, how one group moved from evicting people who are as poor as them to playing soccer in the street and cordoning off the building, and how the other group was left homeless and hopeless after being evicted from the homes they created.

The purpose of this essay is to highlight the housing problem in Johannesburg inner city and how it affects the relationships that people build among each other.

* * *

See photo essay, pp 170–73.

Borrowed by the wind

DAVID MEDALIE

'WHAT'S THE MATTER WITH YOU GUYS?' Jaco demands. 'Or should I say, you girls?'

The group of boys, known as the *main manne*, leans during break against a wall near the Geography room. Herby walks past them on an errand for a teacher and overhears their conversation. He glances at Jaco, who spreads his legs so that his school uniform strains against his powerful limbs.

'Six more months and I'll be defending my country. I can't wait. But you ... you're a bunch of cowards. Wimps. No better than...'

He looks around and spots Herby: '...than him!'

Herby rushes off.

In the distance he hears their laughter. 'I don't think the army would even *take* him,' shouts someone.

He and Jaco never speak directly to each other when they're at school, although – as he did today – Jaco often mocks him. They have almost nothing to do with each other because there's a firm hierarchy. Jaco's at the top: a lion. And he? A field mouse. No, the *turd* of a field mouse.

But there's a big, big secret. Herby hugs it to himself with solemn glee. The joy of it cascades within him. What none of the other boys knows is that he and Jaco are actually friends. They've known each other all their lives – Jaco's family lives on the neighbouring farm – and they spend hours together: in the afternoons, after extra-murals, or on weekends. At school Jaco is little more than a conduit for the predictable views of his father and uncles. But out of school he's different.

Their big secret encloses a smaller one: Jaco – the hero of the rugby field and scorner of bookish boys – likes to read. Herby lends him books, and they discuss them.

'So he's your man?' asks Jaco one day. They're sitting on the dam wall on Jaco's parents' farm, swinging their legs. It's late June, the day before the winter solstice. Everything is dry, the low hills covered with clumps of yellow-tawny grass; but the water in the dam is a blue so vivid it startles the eye. Where they're sitting it's not cold, but the patches of sun are rapidly being apprehended by long, unfolding shadows.

'Who's my man?' Herby is only half-listening. He's relishing yet again their clandestine friendship. He's besotted with the secret itself. He knows that Jaco will never refrain from condemning boys like him when he's with his other friends, but it doesn't matter. When they're alone they never mention the contradiction between the lunging remarks Jaco makes at school and the way he behaves when it's just the two of them. Herby understands that the taunting isn't caused by cruelty in his friend but by something in him. He brings it on himself. The derisory Jaco is merely playing a part. It's not fair to blame the actor for what's in the script.

'DH Lawrence,' says Jaco. 'He's your man, now? No more Kipling?'

'I suppose so.' A puckering wind begins to tug at them. Herby knows this winter wind well, for he's lived on the highveld all his life; and yet every year when it comes he finds that it holds something unfamiliar deep within it. Perhaps it's because its origins are closed to him. He knows not what it knows and has never seen what it has seen. He shivers. Jaco, however, doesn't seem to feel it. As usual, he's dressed in a short-sleeve shirt, shorts and slip-slops.

'What do you like about him?'

'Lawrence? I don't know. I guess ... I guess I like him because he wants the world to be different. And for people to be brave.'

Jaco rubs his chin. 'Well, then you'd better lend me some of his books.'

'Okay, I will.' Herby beams. He loves guiding Jaco's reading. 'I think I'll start you off with some of the short stories, and then...'

'Just don't give me poetry,' Jaco grins at him. It's a standing joke between them: Jaco's willing to read stories and novels, but not poetry.

'Pity. Lawrence's poetry is really good. Listen to this.'

Herby clasps his knees with his arms, closes his eyes and recites the lines in what he considers a sonorous voice:

Not I, not I, but the wind that blows through me!

A fine wind is blowing the new direction of Time.

'Mmm,' says Jaco.

'It comes from a poem called "Song of a man who has come through".'

'What's he come through?'

'Who?'

'That man.'

'I dunno. Life, I suppose.'

'He's lucky. We still got to get through Matric.'

They laugh. A cattle egret lands next to the water's edge and pauses there. Far away a coil of grey smoke rises up. All around them there's a deep silence; a motionlessness, broken only by the scurrying of ripples on the water.

Jaco has left his shirt unbuttoned almost to his midriff and Herby can see the rise of the pectorals and the line of darkish blond hair that trails down his chest. He's haunted by this body. It waylays him in his daydreams and sidles into the visions that come to him at night. Yet,

119

familiar as it is to him, it lures him into a terrain in which he can never find his way. It urges him to follow, leading him down paths darkened by shadows which no one has cast. And as he traipses through this furtive land, he's unsure whether he's an interloper or not.

'I almost forgot to tell you,' Jaco says suddenly, jolting Herby out of his reverie. 'The dogs have killed another blesbuck.'

'Shit.' Herby shakes his head. 'That's bad. Your father must be very upset.'

Jaco's parents farm with game as well as more conventional livestock. In recent weeks three blesbuck have been found dead, their entrails ripped out, but largely uneaten. Jaco's father believes that dogs are the culprits and has blamed those belonging to labourers on Herby's parents' farm – in particular, several families who live close to the perimeter fence.

'How can you be sure it's dogs? Maybe jackals?'

'No, my old man says jackals wouldn't leave the carcass like that. They'd eat it.'

'I suppose he's right.'

'Last night he said I must deal with it. He always does this to me. He makes me do all the crap jobs.'

'Did you tell him you don't want to do it?'

'You know what will happen if I do that.'

Herby nods.

'You wanna come with me?' Jaco has been chewing a blade of grass. He spits it out. 'Tomorrow afternoon?'

'Okay.'

'Great. I'll fetch you just after school.'

The shadows lengthen. 'Aren't you cold?' asks Herby. He looks at Jaco. The late afternoon sun glows on his neck and arms. It looks as if his skin has scooped up the light.

'Nah,' says Jaco. He stands and stretches. 'But I guess it's time to go home.'

The next afternoon, Jaco fetches Herby in his father's bakkie. He's been driving for years – since his legs were long enough to reach the pedals. He's wearing shorts and a tank-top and has exchanged the slip-slops for a pair of boots. The thigh muscles in his left leg bulge whenever he pushes down the clutch.

His mood has changed since yesterday. He frowns as he shades his eyes from the sun with his hand. Herby wonders if there's been an altercation between son and father. He tries to talk to him, but Jaco either says nothing or offers monosyllabic retorts. They've often sat silently together in the past and Herby has always found it companionable. But today the tone of the silence is different: it's ungenerous; and it worries him. He finds himself talking too much.

'Hey,' he says. 'D'you want to hear more of that poem – the one from yesterday?'

Jaco doesn't even look at him.

'DH Lawrence,' says Herby. 'Remember?'

Jaco puts his foot suddenly on the accelerator and the bakkie jerks and then leaps forward.

Herby's heart is beating swiftly. The afternoon, which has barely begun, is already crumbling around him and he doesn't know why it's happening or what to do to make it stop. His mouth is dry and his first attempt at uttering the lines is unsuccessful. *If only ...* he begins, and has to stop and clear his throat. When he finally gets the words out, they sound shrill to him, as if he's 13 years old again and his voice is breaking.

If only, most lovely of all, I yield myself and am borrowed

By the fine, fine wind that takes its course through the chaos of the world

He stops.

'What ... what do you think?'

'Of what?

'Of ... what I've just said.'

Jaco slams on the brakes as the road narrows. The wheels of the bakkie grind against the gravel. On the horizon they can see the huts.

'I told you,' says Jaco. 'Poetry is *kak*. It's for *moffies*.'

The labourers on that part of the farm live in four huts. Three of them are made of mud bricks and corrugated iron, but the fourth, larger than the others, has brick walls and a tiled roof.

Jaco parks a short distance away and strides towards them. Herby follows, a few paces behind. Two dogs rush out as they approach. They're of no identifiable breed. One is brown and the other black and white. The larger of the two, the brown one, barks at them and bares its teeth. The smaller one yaps twice and then backs off.

'Not tied up,' says Jaco, to no one in particular.

A woman and a youth emerge from the biggest hut. The woman nods a greeting. The youth stands next to her.

'Why are these dogs not tied up?' Jaco demands.

'The dogs?' she repeats.

'Yes. Why are they running around? Not tied up?'

'His father not say we must tie them up.' She points at Herby. 'He never say that.'

'They killed the blesbuck on our farm,' Jaco says, raising his voice.

'No' she says. 'They not...'

'They killed our blesbuck.' He holds up three fingers. 'Three dead.'

She says nothing. The youth stares at them. He hasn't moved from his mother's side. In the distance a cow lows and a tractor starts up.

'They go through the fence,' says Jaco, uttering the words slowly, as if counting them, 'and they kill the blesbuck on our farm.'

She shakes her head.

'Don't say no. I'm telling you. I've seen them.'

'Jaco...' Herby feels he must say something. 'I don't think...'

'Shut up!' Jaco turns around and walks back. Herby begins to follow him, but sees that he's bent over the back of the bakkie, reaching for something. He lifts it and returns to them. It's a rifle. The woman covers her mouth with her hand when she sees it.

Herby's heart beats even faster.

'Are you going to tie up the dogs?'

'Please...' she takes her hand away from her mouth and then replaces it.

'It's an easy question,' says Jaco, 'Yes or no?'

There is silence.

'Yes or no?'

No one moves. Jaco holds the gun, pointing it downwards.

Eventually she speaks. 'I must ask his father.' She gestures towards Herby.

'What for? It's our blesbuck.'

'We work on this farm,' says the woman. 'His farm. Not your farm.'

Herby gasps. He knows that nothing can save her now.

Jaco raises the gun and shoots the brown dog. It falls over in the dust and begins twitching. Blood seeps onto the ground from a wound in its neck. The youth rushes towards it, but his mother pulls him back. The black-and-white dog disappears behind one of the huts. Jaco reloads the gun and sets off in pursuit of it. The woman runs after him. 'No,' she calls out. '*Asseblief.*'

Herby can't see what's happening but there's another shot, followed by several high-pitched cries. The gun goes off again and the sounds cease.

Jaco walks swiftly back to the bakkie, tosses the rifle into the back and starts the engine. He drives off while Herby is still getting in.

When they get to the house, he switches off the engine and hunches over the steering-wheel. He groans.

Herby hesitates. 'What's the matter?' he says at last.

'My stomach. Killing me.'

'D'you want to come inside? We might have something.'

'No.'

Jaco doesn't lift his head.

'Are you okay?'

'Not really.'

'Can't believe what you ... can't believe what just happened.'

Herby moves towards him. The gear lever is in the way, but he gets as close to him as he can. Jaco has his head in his arms. He can smell his perspiration. His gaze travels from the back of his neck to the shoulder, all the way down the long arc of the arm.

At that moment everything he has felt and seen throughout the afternoon begins to gather in him. It expands and then tightens until he's left with nothing but an image that draws him inexorably. It's of Jaco, standing in the glare of the winter sun, his legs spread apart, aiming his gun.

As if in a trance he watches his hand move. It strokes the back of Jaco's neck and then moves slowly down his shoulder, down the arm, caressing the skin and the fine blond hairs on the forearm. It rests on the hand. Neither of them moves and they remain like that for what seems like a long time.

Eventually Jaco lifts his head. He looks at Herby's hand as if becoming aware of it for the first time. He shakes his own hand loose and leans across to open the door of the bakkie.

'Out,' he says.

Herby hesitates.

'Now!'

Jaco shoves him out of the bakkie. He bangs his side against the door as he stumbles and falls onto the gravel.

'My father was right about you,' shouts Jaco as he drives away.

As Herby walks down the corridor at school, someone pushes into him and then slams him against the wall. It's Bertus, a thick, loutish boy – a member of Jaco's gang. He grasps Herby around the throat. Other boys surround them and urge Bertus on. Herby tries to see whether Jaco is among them, but there's no sign of him.

'What ... what do you want?' He feels as if the life is being squeezed out of him.

'A little doggie,' says Bertus. 'Two little doggies, in fact. To play with. You can be one of them. I'll stroke you...' – he runs his meaty hand through Herby's hair. 'I'll play with you ... and then ... when I've had enough...'

He punches Herby in the stomach.

He drops to the floor. The boys begin to disperse.

'Leave Jaco alone,' Bertus says. 'He told me what happened

yesterday. Stop bothering him. And stay away from his farm. It's his business what he does there.'

'It was our farm.' Herby can barely get the words out. He's winded. And the revelation of the betrayal has brought bile to his mouth. Gasping, he says, more loudly: 'It was *our* farm.'

But no one hears him.

Grief seeps into him. It's over, he knows. He and Jaco will never exchange another word.

Thirty-one years later Herby receives a Facebook message, accompanied by a request for friendship.

Hey Herby, is that you? the message reads. *Its Jaco. Jaco Kleynhans. How you doing dude? its been a long time. What you been up to?*

He stares. He doesn't know what to do.

Eventually he accepts the request and replies. *Yes, it's me*, he writes. *I'm well, thank you. I hope you are too?*

It soon becomes clear that Jaco doesn't want to spend much time chatting on Facebook. He wants to meet in person, and as soon as possible. Herby lives in Joburg and Jaco in Centurion.

No problem, writes Jaco. *Just tell me where you live. Ill come to your house we got a lot of catching up to do*

On that afternoon, as he waits for Jaco to arrive, he feels apprehensive. He's tired, too: he slept badly the night before, plagued by a dream in which Jaco's adolescent body thrust itself against him in an apocalyptic landscape where children roamed derelict streets, their eyes burning reproachfully.

He wonders how much Jaco remembers of their teenage friendship and what version of it he'll present today. He's puzzled: why has he contacted him after so many years? What does he want? To reminisce about old times? Unlikely. Something to expiate?

A battered-looking car enters the driveway and Jaco emerges. They shake hands and are soon seated in the lounge.

'You got a nice place here,' says Jaco. He's dressed in a creased suit and carries a briefcase. He seems nervous. Herby looks at him. He knew Jaco would have aged; and this is indeed a middle-aged man. But he hasn't aged in the way Herby expected. He imagined greying temples, finely etched crow's feet around the eyes, the same white teeth, bronzed skin stretched more tightly over the same irreproachable bone structure. What he finds instead is disconcerting. The eyes seem to be set much more deeply in the face, the skin is pale in some areas and blotchy in others, and the teeth are rather long and quite unlike the ones he remembers. He looks for the youth he knew, and occasionally he glimpses him: in a phrase, a turn of the lips, a hand resting on the chin. But it's as if that youth has been kept prisoner by an evil scientist who has thickened the past into the present and left the resultant ooze to congeal around the captive.

'You look good,' says Jaco. 'Don't seem to have aged that much. I guess life's treated you well?'

'And you?' Herby responds neither to the compliment nor to the question. He can't reciprocate the former and isn't sure how to answer the latter. 'Has it been good to you?'

'Who can say?' Jaco throws back his head. 'Life's a cunning bitch. Bites you in the arse when you least expect it.'

'Has your family still got the farm?'

'No. We lost it years ago. Before my father died.'

'So what do you do now?'

Jaco seems reluctant to answer. 'I'll get to that a bit later,' he says. 'Let's finish our coffee first. Then we'll have a little chat about that.'

He's divorced, he tells Herby, and struggling to recover financially. 'That cow. She took me to the cleaners.' He's the father of two adult daughters. 'One's got a baby, but she's not married. The other's married to a coloured guy.'

He's a *grandfather*! Herby doesn't comment on that. Instead he says, 'So how do you feel about it? Having a coloured son-in-law?'

'Oh, I'm okay with it.' Jaco takes a pack of cigarettes out of his pocket and looks around the room. When he sees there are no ashtrays, he puts them back in his pocket. 'It's the new South Africa,' he says. 'Everything's changed.'

'But have *you* changed?'

'Totally. Transformed. We have to.'

Herby looks at him, struggling to find more of the old Jaco. But no: the body that at seventeen he knew so well and yet longed to know better offers nothing now but a grotesque incomprehension.

'It's not true of me,' he says. 'Maybe I've changed, yes. But I'm not *transformed.*'

'Oh, I know exactly what you mean.' Jaco winks at him. 'Don't worry about it. We're all racists at heart.'

'No, no. That's *not* what I'm saying. I'm talking about something different.'

'Not sure I'm following.'

Herby doesn't know how best to explain it to him.

'If I'm transformed, if I'm – let's say – a brand new person, then I must have got rid of everything that was inside the old person. But that's not possible.'

Jaco looks even more puzzled.

'Well, here's an example. Violence. It's in me. It's in you. We grew up with it. We could make a decision to get rid of it. But how do we go about doing that?'

'In *you*? But you're not a violent person. You never were.'

'Violence isn't just a way of hurting people. It's also a form of knowledge. And very hard to unlearn. Look at South Africa today.'

'Whoa,' says Jaco, 'this is getting too deep for me. Way too deep. You always thought too much about things.' He reaches for his briefcase. 'But you know, Herby, all this talk of life and death and what's-it-all-about is actually more to the point than you realise.' He produces several pamphlets and puts them on the coffee table. 'I want to tell you something,' he says. 'Old friends are special. And what are you? My oldest friend in the world. So I want to do something special for you. Take my word for it: opportunities like this don't come along every day. I'm going to introduce you to a unique product. It's a privilege to share it with you.'

It's Herby's turn to be puzzled.

'All will be revealed,' says Jaco. 'Just give me a little more of your time and I'll explain everything. Come, sit next to me.'

Herby has to sit very close to Jaco as they pore together over the pamphlets. The proximity makes him uneasy. Jaco used to smell of sun and sweat; it was a rank, unapologetic smell, and it thrilled Herby. Now he smells of stale, sweet aftershave and cigarette smoke. Strong as these odours are, they're also diffident, suppressed. It's as if there's something lurking within the body that exudes them that has made it become ashamed of its own needs.

Later, Herby walks Jaco to the car. He promises to think it over. 'I never had any interest in buying life insurance,' he finds himself saying. 'Never even thought about a policy. But, as you say, one never knows...'

'It's important to think of the future. After all, my friend, we're not getting any younger. Hell, we could keel over any minute.' Jaco puts his briefcase in the boot and gets into the car. 'And as you said yourself, we live in a violent place. Danger around every corner. Who knows what might happen tomorrow?' He brandishes an imaginary gun, points it at his temple, and curls his finger to indicate pulling the trigger. 'At the risk of repeating myself: it's a great deal. I wouldn't have brought it to you if it wasn't. I only chose you because we go back such a long way.'

'We sure do.'

Jaco gets into the car and rolls down the window.

'You'll thank me one day,' he says.

'I thank you now.'

They shake hands.

'Hey,' says Jaco. 'Still reading DH Lawrence?'

'No. Haven't read him in years.'

'What do you read now?'

'Different things. Quite a lot of South African literature.'

'No more British books?'

'Oh, yes. From time to time.'

'Such as?'

'Well … I like Hollinghurst.'

'What's that?'

'Alan Hollinghurst. He's a contemporary writer.'

'Never heard of him. Any good? I'll borrow some of his books from you – if you think I'll like it.'

He turns on the engine and pumps the accelerator several times. Fumes pour out of the exhaust pipe.

'He's good,' says Herby. 'You won't like it.'

'Ah, well.' Jaco waves at him. 'Cheers, my friend. You've got my number now. Don't be a stranger. Look at that material I left you and call me. Soon. We can't wait another 30 years.'

Herby waves back at him.

Jaco begins to reverse out of the driveway. He stops and beckons Herby to come closer.

'You know, memories are funny things,' he says. 'Seeing you today … so much is coming back to me. D'you remember that poem – about the man who came through?'

'Of course.'

'I really liked it,' he says.

'Did you?'

'It was good. But it means more to me now. We knew nothing then. Bugger-all. We thought we were *groot manne*, but we were babies. I found that out when I went to the army. What a shit time that was, hey?'

'I never went to the army.'

'How come?'

'It's a long story. I'll tell you another day.'

'Well, it was lousy.'

'I'm sure.'

Jaco takes his hands off the steering-wheel and runs them through his hair. 'Okay. So tell me, Herby.'

'Tell you what?'

'It's 30 years later. I want to know. Are you a man who's come through?'

Herby pauses.

He's astonished to discover how moved he is by the question; almost to tears.

'I ... I'm not sure. Are you?'

'You betcha!' He puts the car into reverse again. 'I'm a survivor,' he yells above the noise of the engine. 'I've been down but I'm not out.'

He hoots twice before driving off.

Herby rushes back into the house. He can't wait to throw away the pamphlets. He even takes them to the outside bin. He doesn't want them in his house for one more minute. They're a source of contagion, of that he's certain. What they'll infect him with, he cannot say; but infect him they will.

He replays the visit several times in his head, going over all the gaps in Jaco's conversation and the apparent chasms in his recollections. The lack of interest in his own life he can set aside, but not what Jaco has done to the past. He seems to think it belongs solely to him; that he can make of it whatever he likes. It's so ... what's the right word? So *cynical*. Cowardly too. And it's not just him. People do it all the time: borrowing from the past what they can never replace and imputing promises to it which they know it cannot keep. He tried to bait Jaco – especially with the reference to violence – but it didn't work. In the end he let him get away with it.

He goes into the garden and sits on a bench. The sun is about to set. He hears frogs croaking near the koi pond. His neighbours are having cocktails: there's laughter and the clinking of glasses.

In this soft preparation for night, the afternoon gives way. Herby yields to it and, as he does so, he finds himself beginning to release his tight grip on what happened earlier.

This Jaco he met today isn't deliberately defiling the past. He's ransacking it, rifling through the long-ago days in a desperate attempt to find anything which may be of advantage to him. Even if he remembers precisely how their friendship ended, it's not in his interest to recall it.

What's more: it's too easy to blame him for everything. Too easy and too glib. After all, he was waging his own battles with his father.

Yes, Jaco used to abuse him; but he allowed it. He knew exactly what he was doing.

Yes, Jaco shot the dogs; but it was he, Herby, who turned what he witnessed into a tableau. It was he who grafted desire onto what happened that day.

Almost imperceptibly the shadows find a new direction. Objects lose their outlines as the light marbles into violet and cream.

In jail

THANDOKUHLE MNGQIBISA

In jail
Blue is always drunk. Stumbles back to the yard. Gumption in her mouth, Full enough to choke on.

Dances dizzy
To her favourite crush.
Slurs 'honey, let mama show you some real love'. Flashes her knickers,
Pays no mind her dejected arms.

Blue is a curtain.
Let's the wind and the sun flutter inside. Keeps grubby whispers from my palms.
She's a safe space when I don't want to be watched. When the wrong sort force their eyes past,
She is waiting, guard.

She keeps my inside.
Dirt and mess and smiles.
And ends up in jail, to keep me alive

Becomes the rusty metal frame of the bed. The leaky plumbing.

So I sneak wine into visitation
And we pretend we're having a picnic,
In 2016;
On my living room floor
Before she slit that man's throat to save me

Things that will get you beaten in a black home
Telling the Truth

THANDOKUHLE MNGQIBISA

In the taxi a four-year-old excitedly watches
This chorus of economy
Everyone seems to know the notes to the song
Send quiet money forward
Get noisy money back
She tries to count how many sweets a rainbow can buy
Or better yet, a clinking coin
As soon as the aria is over
She sits bored
In the silence now, she shouts
Mama, siyaphi singagezanga?[20]

---

20 Mama, where are we going when we haven't bathed?

Drowning

❧

THANDOKUHLE MNGQIBISA

* * *

See photo essay, pp 174–75.

'Your kink is not my kink'

African queer women and gender non-conforming persons find sexual freedom in bondage

SIPHUMEZE KHUNDAYI &
TIFFANY MUGO

AFRICAN CULTURES HAVE LONG CELEBRATED sexuality, with a history filled with customs and traditions dedicated to pleasure, sexual satisfaction and sex being seen as a social good. However, the moral frameworks of religions such as Christianity and Islam as well as notions of nationalism have in many cases submerged indigenous practices aimed at honouring and celebrating sex. There has become a serious disconnect in how we engage with ideas of sex and sexuality framing ideas around morality and warning signs about the impending doom that comes with seeing people naked.

However, issues of pleasure and bodily autonomy are again beginning to take centre stage. This is evident in the increasing number of public platforms and initiatives dealing with women's sexual agency. For example, platforms such as *Adventures from the Bedrooms of African Women* and *The Spread Podcast* centralise pleasure as a principle. The focus on African pleasure is not limited to the online space. Works like *Pussy Print*, by Lady Skollie, who is a feminist artist and activist from South Africa, and the Safe Sex and Pleasure (#PleaseHer) workshops by HOLAAfrica! also tackle what gets people off and what it means to control your body in wildly different ways.

It is no surprise then that new conversations about Kink are thriving on the continent – led by an unapologetic generation of queer black women. Indeed, there is an active Bondage Discipline/Dominance Sadism/Submission Masochism (BDSM) scene that is a site of pleasure, activism and academic enquiry for a queer community coming into its own in a context characterised both by state repression and pockets of social openness.

Over the past couple of years Siphemeze Khundayi, the co- creator of this piece, and I have had an increasing personal and professional interest in kink. It all begun shortly after an 'Erotica Justice' dialogue, which was held under the banner of HOLAAfrica, a sex positive organisation we founded. The space was created to look at how the revolution could be taken out of streets and put in the sheets. The dialogue used the starting point that sex is an important part of bodily autonomy, so people spoke about the kind of sex they were having – the good, the bad, the problematic and the mundane.

At one point Tshegofatso, who had long been an online fave, held the floor and spoke about how BDSM was based on consent, how it needed a constant discussion of wants, needs and desires. To understand your partner/s and their engagement with you and your body.

The room lost its collective mess.

'No way!' They cried. 'Kink is privileged sex!' they exclaimed. 'These are things for the middle class/white people.' 'Where is the feminism and autonomy in kink?'

By the end of the conversation we were intrigued by this sexual practice that seemed to be a delicious dichotomy. We also wanted to know why the very notion of kink had been rejected by most of the people in the room. We wanted to know what we could learn from this sexual practice that was often ignored in other sexual practices. We wanted to know why there was so much leather involved and was it practical with the amount of sweating that happens when you have sex. But the main question was: should we try kink?

And so we began to have conversations, develop think pieces, gather the observations of friends, practiced and allowed ourselves to be taught how to kneel and submit over WhatsApp and during dinner parties. We sought relationship advice based on bondage.

All of this began to form a core part of the work of HOLAAfrica with photo shoots, posts on our site and even our #PleaseHer safe sex and pleasure manual which archived all of this knowledge.

This essay is part of that wet and wild journey to understanding something outside our initial comfort zones. This research was one of the first steps down the rabbit hole. Within this project we reached out to some of the kinksters we had met since embarking on this journey. Siphumeze drew from the archive of photos she had taken of various queer women. The work sought to add to the increasingly changing conversation within the Sexual Reproductive Health Rights narrative, moving the conversation away from more traditional notions of HIV/AIDS, Female Genital Mutilation and child marriage.

SUBBING WHILST BLACK

One can imagine that there are general problems of SWB (subbing whilst black). Given the historical constructions of black women's sexualities and the present-day violence that continues to be marshalled against black women both across the continent and in the diaspora, it is not a stretch to imagine that in entering an interracial BDSM situation black queer women might be inundated with images straight out of a documentary on colonisation or slavery. Even in sexual interactions that do not involved interracial contact, the history and reality of social expectations regarding women's submissiveness make this – at first appearance – a complex space to manage.

So why would a black queer woman and or a gender non-conforming person *consider* BDSM let alone find intimacy, joy and pleasure in acts that evoke ideas of violence and bondage, and that require submission. Yet it is precisely the ability to navigate this nexus of pain, risk, pleasure and protection that many queer women on the scene seek.

POWER AND CONSENT: AN AGE-OLD BATTLE

In her *Vice* piece '*The power of being a black woman in bed*', Michelle Ofiwe says 'growing up, I realized that I encountered few narratives of tender Black women.' She muses about how the perception that black women are 'strong' can make it difficult for them to vocalise and accept vulnerability. Within BDSM the notion of power – who has it, who to give it to and when to hold it – are central to the sex act.

Ofiwe points out there is a freedom in exploring new ways of sex and pleasure, a queering of interactions that subverts and explores notions that are taken for granted within more mainstream 'vanilla' notions of sex.

Muthoni, a queer activist from Kenya, unpacks the role of BDSM in helping heal scars caused by sexual violence. She says, 'It heals the history around the woman's place in sex as a recipient, therefore the sole purpose of a man's pleasure. BDSM gives the woman the agency to clearly define and negotiate their power.'

For Muthoni, 'It's liberating to up notions of power in a trusting space.' She explains that the ability to negotiate the sex that you want is empowering and liberating. Being a queer woman from East Africa, safety is a constant negotiation. There is a need to compromise your bodily autonomy all the time. BDSM forces you to say 'yes'. It makes you agree on the rules. It rewards you for asking for more when you want it and for saying stop when you don't. Even as power is central to BDSM, so too are trust and consent. That's where the pleasure lies. As Muthoni concludes, 'BDSM demands that sex and power is mutual and shared willingly and honestly.'

Kgothatso, a queer woman based in southern Africa, says 'rope reminds me of the liberation I find in BDSM. It reminds me that there is much freedom in being able to relinquish all control.'

It is both in being able to be in control and at the same time relinquishing control that these women can explore their ability to negotiate power. Although there are assumptions that the kink scene is about imposed pain and violence, the reality is force is not the rule in BDSM interactions. Instead, when it does occur, it is 'an unwanted exception'.[21]

Consent is defined as 'informed agreement between persons to act in an activity which is mutually beneficial for everybody involved'. Whereas in heteronormative sexual interactions, consent is often riddled with grey areas, in kink, it is essential that these issues are addressed head on. Because pleasure and pain are bound together, kinksters are generally meticulous in addressing the boundaries.

Tshegofatso, a sex positive blogger, feels strongly about this. 'Kink is all about consent. Within the kink world I have felt I have the power to consent more than I have in every other aspect,' she says. For her consent is one of the most important and central parts of the kink experience. Tshegofatso considers sexual growth and knowledge fundamental parts of BDSM. She says she was lucky to be exposed to kinksters who conceptualised consent in a way that made her feel safe and able to explore her desires. She explains: 'When comparing that [engagement with consent] to non kinksters I have been able to find a lot more control and a lot more able to experiment with things that previously had been uncomfortable with as I know in the kink world I am constantly learning.'

---

21 A. Fulkerson, 'Bound by consent: Concepts of consent within the leather and bondage, domination, sadomasochism (BDSM) communities' (2010).

When one considers that at the core of BDSM are the notions of consent, openness, transparency and trust, one can see why this realm would allow so many women to reclaim sexual desire and autonomy. It is also evident why the practice is queer – it is too liberating, too grounded in choice and equality to form a part of patriarchally defined sex practices.

SEXUAL EXPLORATION: PINPOINTING PLEASURE

One of the most confronting and liberating aspects of BDSM is the fact that typical gender roles and ideas of sexuality do not apply to BDSM. One of the women I interviewed – Thabile, a South African lesbian – stated, 'Kink simply allows me to be without judgement.' She emphasised that kink allows her to explore what feels good to her and take it as far as she wants to, and then allows her to stop if that's what she wants to do too.

Thabile explains that for her kink 'is a safe space of exploration and just being. A space where expectations are clear and worked towards, not just by yourself but with other people that care to learn you and work on keeping you safe.' She explains that, 'There are a lot of dynamics in life that one cannot control.' For Thabile, 'the stripping of control also means the limiting of how one expresses themselves; so my involvement in kink is me trying to learn about myself in an environment that enables authenticity and the ability to just be damn right honest.'

BDSM gives women tools and a framework for clearly defining and negotiating their needs and their limits.

For these queer women the space is one in which they can delve into what makes them feel good, what gets them off, what sexually excites them and what they consider to be safe sexual engagements within a healthy, cognitive and communicative framework.

CONCLUSION

In private conversations and in their public art and media initiatives African queer women's explorations of BDSM are subverting dominant narratives about who owns pleasure, who can dictate what happens to another person's body and what good sex looks like. Through acts of submission and domination they are reclaiming their bodily autonomy and their right to sex that is safe, empowered and pleasurable. Queer women are choosing what feels good and what is good. In a time and space where many women are not able to take sexual pleasure for granted, this is a rare privilege.

The private (and public) conversations about sex lead us to understand that different notions are central to the experience of pleasure, sexuality, sensuality and the erotic. As each of the women profiled above demonstrate, it is agency that makes sex so delicious. Queer women find a sensuous experience in kink – like when you are eating the exact meal that you want and sharing it with the dinner guests of your choosing.

Note: Thank you to the queer women who aided in the compilation of the ideas and quotes for this paper and those who gave their beautiful bodies for the images. You stay magic.

* * *

See photo essay, pp 176–83.

XXYX Africa

More Invisible

NICK HADIKWA MWALUKO

PART ONE

ON THE SUBJECT OF VOICING THAT inner scream that is your song...

LGBT Africa held two truths: you fuck, you die. Both truths were intimately woven like tapestry spun by a wild heart against an overreaching national government bracketed from the world stage, answerable solely to itself, wielding unmolested corrupted powers. If caught, the government had every right to kill you, shoot you dead-on-the-spot or torture you by electrocuting your vagina, penis slow but steady as water was poured so the amplified shock proved so lethal you'd fry to death for quick bodily disposal; if lucky, you fucked like you might die. Meaning with intensity, not wasting that urge to connect with someone of the same sex who shared your wish to be

ALIVE, truly ALIVE because what proved to be deadly was living a lie every day.

Third World fucking is hard-core sex zero nonsense: we sucked, swallowed, dicked, gulped, licked, fingered, penetrated, moaned, groaned, grunted, squirted, sprinkled, dribbled, bent down, bent over, spread wide, even wider, head-down-ass-up, swallow-every-drop-nonstop whenever and wherever nobody was watching, and if they did chance a glimpse, we fucked even harder, not wasting a drop of love or life or the scraps of sex pieced together in zero-time with a loaded gun at your skull.

Healing powers were summoned to quiet that extra-crispy brand of brutality reserved especially for queer Africans. We licked the death-wish within the body's hidden caverns, our skilled African tongues glossing over bruises from beatings – pipes, stones, Daddy's belt while your mother watched in stunned silence. We seduced delicious poetry from crushed glass inserted deep within a young lesbian's tight vagina so her rapist could make her 'less gay' to make her more of a 'traditional African woman' who preferred 'real African men' to masculine women. When it was over it was never over. If you survived, you crawled into the shadows where your scream against Death hit pitch-fever, head back howling your warning so the community might paint a future through your sound. We never saw ourselves on TV; never heard our stories on radio; never held parades to celebrate hard-won struggles against relentless, day-after-day oppression; had no materials, no paraphernalia, no lube nor tube; no twelve-inch, uncut, jet-Black dildo with glow-in-the-dark sprinkles to decorate your plastic cock; no flag, no label, no symbol, no language, no code, no metaphor, no books, no song; no shops, no clubs, no bars; no celebrated space to pour our souls into alternative realities.

No church or sacred community prayed over us or blessed gay people because they said we have no souls. We were invisible, that unreality within reality, a truth so true that when we first appeared they said we were a lie. The ones who couldn't take it anymore, the ones who refused to stay silent or hide, the few brave ones who stood up to declare themselves openly gay and proud Africans became too gay, meaning unAfrican. It was instant. They were disowned by family, dumped by lovers, denied by community, spat on by the ancestors, they went from office workers with (decent) salaries to bums fishing garbage from dumpsters, roaming the streets as sex workers prostituting for tourists to get by hand-to-mouth – if they were lucky.

Too quickly, they got that wild look of someone pushed far out on the edge. Suddenly, the thin line between sanity and insanity was a teetering question of time. Nobody reached out to help or hope – too risky – so they wasted away in distant lands pimped by some mysterious blue-eyed tourist, returning home with HIV, then dumped in the backwoods of their village to die a slow, painful death in disgraced anonymity.

Our very first foot soldiers were heroes and sheroes and tranny-oes who sang their noble song, risking Life's preciousness to voice a more precious truth. LGBT Africans armed with beautiful queernesses prepared to die for an ideal, unprepared to force-fuck heterosexuals in exile, stunned when they returned and were treated like strangers at home in their own motherland. They did not die from HIV/AIDS; NO!NO!NO!, they died from loneliness. Acute isolation sapped their strength, took away their ability to rise beyond the grave and reclaim the queer bodies so proudly declared before the world from Alpha into Omega, beginning from their end.

In the end, they never knew their worth to their own community; but we know it and we will sing it forever, proclaiming eternity as we reach for Infinity where queer Africa lives forever and ever, Ase.

For us few watchful survivors on the side-lines, the village sent a clear message: 'Fight back, you will fall. Fall, nobody will catch you. Die, no ancestor will receive your rotten, gay body in the hereafter where judgement is even worse.' We looked in the mirror, measured our stubborn pride and saw death. It's that look you get when you don't stand in your own truth, when you spin lies to fuel dreams that account for your emotional isolation. We were safer and yet hypocrites; wounded survivors too lost, too confused to trust or risk beyond the paralysing fear that had us actively stuck in a loveless world: in other words, we were not ourselves. We broke down, cried like infants – motherless, vulnerable, unwanted, abandoned, craving. Rather than unravel, rather than end up crazy or strapped to some bed locked away for life in a mental institution because some medical 'expert' had determined we were 'too insane' to live in a world that wished us death, rather than end up in prison or sentenced to life in an asylum, rather than lose what little power we gained through tears and precious bloodshed and deep love, we decided to stay invisible; YES, yes, we worked really, really hard to make ourselves absolutely nothing. 'Better safe', we thought, so we played at being 'normal', 'ordinary', 'average', 'nice'; we made ourselves 'predictable', 'routine', 'stale', 'flat', modelled our behaviour after 'good citizens' who worship the grave. We fabricated shallow but necessary lies, swallowed spoonfuls of phobia to stay safe inside the cosy closet.

We looked at each other sideways if at all. 'Wide-eyed blind' is what I call it, when you look not to see someone but to make sure they stay invisible. Easy enough: how do you identify when your process involves erasing so much of yourself? We betrayed each other, hurt each other, cursed, destroyed each other, then worked extra hard to caress the special wounds birthed by extra-crispy cruelty; by internalised oppression. And we drank – too, too much – liquor plus laughter bubbling tonic during troubled times. Suddenly, one bright morning, everything broke: the sun rose high to cast penetrating light on our lies but they were gone, had disappeared; that false, artificial ring in our voice sounded true, even authentic; plastic gestures that made us normal became natural; we were masters of this world and its pathetic, shallow, stupid standards. So we were comfortable, yes, finally safe. Next day, we were still safe and just as plastic. Following day, still fake and safe. Next day, more fake, more shallow, less alive. Then, finally, we were too safe because were too fake because we were too dead.

More fake, more safe; more safe, less alive; less alive, more dead; more dead, more artificial; more artificial, more insincere; more insincere, more accommodating; more accommodating, more polite; more polite, more approved of; more approved of, more accepted; more accepted, more connected; more connected, more alienated; more alienated, more alone; more alone, more lost; more lost, more confused; more confused, more scared; more scared, less secure; less secure, more insecure; more insecure, more drinking; more drinking, more drugs, more drugs, more numb; more numb, more lies; more lies, more artificial; more artificial, more fake; more fake, more safe; more safe, less alive; less alive, more dead; more dead, too dead; too dead, too safe. Such was the formula.

Is this the cure?

There is a war between my legs. It keeps me pure. To reach out and touch someone who touches me back fuels the frenzy feeding my lust. To touch the throne where African miracles are queer. To celebrate the tension between existence and being alive. Beyond impossible, taking step after carefully crafted step, to enter that spatial reality where nothing breathes and everything is alive. To hold the sun. To be the light. To kiss infinity with my eyes. Living inside someone for limited eternity, Love defeats death, my soul defeats my mind, scars scream when pain is shared, our chaos is a perfect symphony. When partnered it means someone is out there, another African just as starved for love and life. Maybe, just maybe a tribe is in my future if I survive the (present) moment. If I claim the body that holds the story to voice my song, if I taste the death-wish, swallow the bullet during illegal fucking, if I re-imagine the world behind my eyelids, recreating reality to make it mine, aaaall mine. In a world committed to making sure every queer African goes crazy, when I choose to look beyond the world, beyond circumstance in search of an identity, have I done everything in my power to meet this moment? Isn't this why some of us refuse to hide? Don't I like myself more when living in integrity? Am I more alive?

Countdown to BOOM.

Five ...

Four ...

Three ...

It's night time. Even though I sleep on my stomach to hide my vagina, they find it, flip me over. With both hands, I cover my hairy mound, thinking, my T-cock (Transsexual cock) will go mega-penis as an act of resistance. Prayer: Dear Penis, I will not get wet so don't betray me. Listen, do not, I repeat, don't you dare participate or orgasm during my sexual assault or I will drown in a merciless river called queer shame, understood? In the name of the Father, the Son, the Holy Spirit and my Ancestors, Ase.

Two ...

One ...

Breaking news: Prominent Ugandan LGBT activist David Kato was found dead in his home following repeated blows to the head and skull with a hammer.

One guy rapes my asshole doggy style; one guy rapes my mouth; one guy rapes my T-hole-vagina.

Kato, a schoolteacher and advocacy officer for Sexual Minorities Uganda (SMUG), won a lawsuit against a magazine that published his name and photograph on its front pages, outing him as a gay man and calling for his execution.

My rape feels so alive and yet unreal. From those depths of numb confusion my revolutionary truth is born, yes, screams powerful as egg yolk morph into my chant poetry: I refuse to be a woman for them I refuse to be a woman for them I refuse to have a gender I refuse to have a gender I refuse to have a body I refuse to have a body. I refuse to take ownership of my existence. My body is not their dumping ground, nor is it a grave for their sick, twisted pleasure. My body will not house nor be a sanctuary for toxic masculinity. I refuse to participate, own, or claim their reality. I am not your victim, survivor, warrior. I will not bow to patriarchy. I will not apologise. 'No to hate,' I say, '"yes" to love.' No to stereotype; no to (gender) roles; no to your rigid, inhuman compartments. No to the gender police, thought police, border patrol. My body is the first frontier for resistance. I refuse to honour concepts of time and space blind to our generational trauma. I refuse to cement the power of intimacy with a shared language.

Kato's alleged murderer, a male sex worker, was denounced by local and international activists as a scapegoat used by government authorities to fuel false links between homosexuality, deviancy and criminality.

Failure, helplessness, vulnerability are my core superpowers. In the affirmative, yes I come from dust and to dust I willingly return.

David Kato was 47 years old when he died.

At this point, this moment of complete surrender/ surrender/ surrender, when I know nothing because I am nothing, and because I am nothing all I know is nothing, this is where divine intelligence becomes revelation. I flirt with it. The penis raping my mouth transitions into a hot queer trans-lesbian's pussy raping my tongue back and forth. S/he sticks hyr fingers inside my asshole, vagina, moving within spatial realities only queers of colour crack. Touch is the real revolution, a letter to my lovers. I am We. And We are many genders, as many as there are people on the planet, each orgasm signalling the birth of new nebula. Another cosmic reality, another world, another Self speaking another language yes my body is not a prison my body is not a prison my body is not a prison queer lesbian fuck-fest was born to transcend, to take back the power stripped from us before time began. Such is the manifesto tattooed on my heart.

BOOM!

We are queer, we are here[22]

CHIBỤÌHÈ OBI

1

THE FIRST TIME I FELT COMPELLED TO document the queer body in my writing was during my second year at university. I had this toe-curling experience at the hostel one night that left me tugging at my pen and bleeding profusely into the banality of an empty piece of paper from the midnight when the fracas broke out until around five in the morning when it all ended. I wanted to register my protest, to enter, as a witness, what I saw that night. But, when the first light flashed through the window that morning, I discovered the sheet of paper had largely remained blank save for the weight of water that had seeped through and left smudges across its face. Unbeknownst to me, I had not been writing. What bled throughout that night was not ink; was not letters. It was tears – my body unhinged by the wounds inflicted on it, the

---

22   First publisher by *Brittle Paper* on 17 May 2017.

narrative of silence foisted upon its porous terrain. It was tears. Every alphabet, every language resident in my consciousness, had taken flight and the rest became melted anguish; became hot, clammy tears.

This was what happened.

The guy living across my room had been marked out – identified as gay – by this gang of boisterous boys. They had searched for the best time to pick him without stirring much dust. So that night – because it was the first week of a new semester and students were yet to resume fully – they came for him. They kick open the wooden door shielding him and dragged him into the open. They hit him repeatedly with whatever objects they felt would break him and call forth confessions.

Boots, balled fists, sticks, slaps. They asked him who and who were gay. They asked him to name names. There was no way it could be only him. They wanted to purge the hostels of fucking faggots and liberate the entire school from the infestation of ass-swinging taboos.

But this guy was not cooperative. He would not squeal; did not confess.

Like other queer people on campus, he had tried to be invisible. When you fall into a species that has been marked as odd; a species isolated as foreign, as not belonging and therefore as being dangerous and deserving death, you learn how to hide, how to be invincible, how to disappear. For every one of the days I had known him over the year we had been together at school, his had been a life wrapped carefully in layers of fear. Each step he took was a study in apology, every gesture a prayer cautiously whispered into the air.

But that night, all those careful layers he had laboured to construct gave way as knives slashed into his body. Every cut was followed by a scream. The sound of his torture kept me clutching the pen with an urgency I had not known before. No one came to his rescue that night, and after it was all over, no one cared to ask what became of him either. Not the school security guard who hounded around; not the students who poured out of their rooms, excitement kicking like wild horses in their stomachs. Not even me; holed up in my room gripped with fear, unable to write and very, very uncertain of my own fate.

Now, I think of that incident and that night and I am confronted with the truth. The reason I could not write into that piece of paper that night was this: there was no audience for the type of narrative I was about to spin – a narrative where the queer body is documented as wronged, as deserving of justice. There was no such readership. Our school was a secure community where, like every part of this country, the dominant narrative about gays was (and still is) negative. Gays are monsters, they are beasts to be exterminated by whatever crude means. The queer body deserved any form of violence meted out against it.

ll

> Is it not astonishing to contemplate how this body that loves
> other men began the century imprisoned and broken and ends
> the century tortured, lashed to fences and torched on a pyre of
> automobile tires in a junkyard.
> – CLIFF BOSTOCK

Mob attacks on homosexuals, or even perceived homosexuals, in Nigeria are not new. They have always been part of the news, and for a country where jungle justice is rife and where homosexuals are common enemy across religious and cultural groups, homophobic violence is as rampant as it is frequent.

The headlines are full of stories. 'Two homosexuals were lynched yesterday at Lagos mainland.' Or. 'A gay man burnt in Onitcha or Aba'. Or. 'A homosexual hide out was discovered and raided in Sokoto. The eight identified members have been tried by the sharia court and will be stoned to death.'

In the age of the Internet, violence against the queer body has taken a different dimension. It is no longer enough to lynch or burn them. The assailants aided by the homophobic majority and a culture bent on eradicating every trace of homosexuality go on to mock and defame their burnt or lacerated bodies.

On 17 February 2016, Akin, a gay man, was lynched by a homophobic mob in Ondo state, Nigeria. Social media was agog.

Stories flew around. Once again, the queer body came under intense scrutiny and became the centre of attention. Akin's body, mapped with machete cuts, bleeding from his skull was portrayed as deserving of violence. As he lay in critical condition in hospital, the comments on his Facebook timeline spewed hatred. 'This will teach others a great lesson.' The subtext was clear: 'Oh you sick queers, behold him and see what bitter fate awaits you all.'

Bloggers and journalists placed this in perspective. How else could the public sharing of Akin's bashed body be explained? Where his assailants had stopped in their mission to humiliate the queer body, Facebook users and bloggers had continued by hitting the share button. No, it was not out of pity. Not because they wished to get justice for Akin, or immunity for the many Akins waiting for their turns; waiting to be happen. Their intentions were neither humanistic nor altruistic. No, they were voyeurs, watching the punishment of a queer body, egging on the assailants; standing on the moral high ground while they pushed gays off a cliff.

lll

I've longed to find dignified and respectful depictions of queers in Nigerian literature. To search for one's self in literature and to not find yourself; or to find that you are perpetually twisted and shunned and vilified is a different sort of violence. Nigeria's literary culture has not been fair to the queer body. It has not been fair to the queer narrative. There are holes and gaps, gullies no one is willing to examine.

Queer themes are rarely incorporated into literary discourses; it is ridiculous to believe Nigeria is a country without queers; that the many cultures comprising the giant of Africa have no place for gays, for kink, for women who are strong and men who are too pretty. With the exception of Jude Dibia and Chinelo Okparanta, writers exploring queer themes mostly approach queer stories from the fringes.

Queer poetry was almost non-existent until recently, until Amatesiro Dore, until Romeo Oriogun, until myself – and this is because Ainehi Edoro began to publish us in *Brittle Paper*. Before that, publishers rejected our poems not because they were poorly written but because in our poems we were not ashamed of our queerness; of our queer bodies, or our queer lives; of our love. Some butchered our work in the most callous and savage manner in their bid to silence our queer voices.

But we have refused to be silenced.

We have refused invisibility.

The only way to change this narrative is to document our own experiences as queer writers or writers of queer literature as the case may be. We must tell our own stories – stories of our gorgeous bodies and the pains and scars inflicted on them by the homophobic society in which we live.

In their introduction to *Queer History, Queer Now*, Cecca Ochoa and Alejandro Varela emphasise that 'so much history is lost, so much exists as whispers and rumors. We must document our own histories, or we risk a mis-telling and an opportunity for justice in truth.' We must reject silence, shun invincibility, and strive not to give in to compromise. We must be ready to pay the high price.

Romeo Oriogun's electronic poetry chapbook, *Burnt Men*, published by Praxis magazine was the first attempt to document the horrific experience of living as a queer person in Nigeria. When I was contacted to shoot a photograph for the cover last year, I knew that the journey to heal the queer body and redeem the narrative had begun. Between the publication of that chapbook and now, some fabulous things have happened. Our queer bodies are healing and rising and coming out of the dark places where they have been confined for far too long. Our queer bodies are crawling out of obscurity. The queer anthology, *14: We Are Flowers*, is us basking in the sun. Romeo Oriogun's recent Brunel Prize win sees us shouting loud and clear. 'We are here.'

Before this moment, everything has been struggle and suffocation. It has been silence and invisibility. There were days I felt so lost, so displaced that I felt smaller than a panting, gasping organism, reaching and yet damaged, deliberately pushed towards extinction. There were days I walked into this room called Nigerian Literature and read stories, perused its themes and interests and wanted to scream. Where am I? Once or twice I chanced upon images of us, but usually we were behind a curtain, beaten and violated, screaming for attention and inclusion. Asking to be let in.

But of course this recent visibility has led to opposition. The price of freedom is always resistance. And I write this with the literary community in mind.

Sometime last year, I was invited to do a reading at Imo State University (IMSU) by a literary society there. During the reading, a section of the audience became incensed by the homoerotic inclination of my poems. Egged on by a certain Johnbosco Chukwuebuka, a writer with a handful of books to his credit, they began to yell and scream. They threatened to call the police if I didn't stop. The reading was halted amid threats of arrest and hostility.

Then, two weeks after the Owerri Book Festival, an unknown young man followed me to the rear gates of IMSU. When he finally caught up with me, he threatened to cut off my penis if I continued to write and promote homosexuality.

The organisers of the book festival had asked me to talk about the queer body in literature, but the discussion had ended in chaos.

It is over a year now since poems exploring queer identity began to appear in Nigeria's literary spaces. Threats have been coming. Thick-brained humans come to my Facebook inbox and write long sermons peppered with hate and warnings. One said I should seek home elsewhere because Nigeria will not tolerate my needs and clamour. Another asked Romeo to send him some money or he'd send policemen after him.

One Sunday evening in April, Romeo contacted me to say that someone had reported him to the police near his new post. The officers called to inform him that they would be at his office soon to arrest him. We were able to avert the arrest, because it was baseless. Still, the threat and the harassment are psychologically draining.

Last August, I received a death threat on my phone via WhatsApp.

I have stopped making public my locations on social media. If I need to, I register my presence long after I have left the place. I try to keep my movements discrete. This way I have been able to forestall any premeditated attack.

The threats are becoming overwhelming. I do not speak only for myself. I speak for every queer voice that stands outside and yet tries to speak into the Nigerian literary space. I speak for Romeo Oriogun. I speak for Pwaangulongii Dauod whose house was invaded. The threats are no longer confined to social media; they have bled into our lives, into the real and the physical, into actual rooms we occupy, jobs we hold, cafés we frequent. We are not metaphorically afraid – we are physically, literally under threat.

We are the ones left holding the fear long after the hashtags and the social media solidarity.

And so, we are the ones who must proclaim that queer literature is a legitimate component of Nigerian, nay African, literature. We must scream from the rooftops, and from the shacks and shanties we have called home, we must say that queer literature is a subtext of the whole. Queer literature is part of the story, part of the struggle, part of the style and syntax. Queer literature matters, and queer writers and artists matter equally within the Nigerian literary community.

It has come to stay. We're queer and we're here.

Reclamation[23]

HAPUA ONONIME

ON 19 JUNE LAST YEAR, I WAS KIDNAPPED by a gang that held me for a day until my parents paid a ransom. For weeks afterwards, I lived in a kind of self-induced fear as a result of the footage they took of me, naked. I remember lying on the ground, not able to remember the exact answer I had given them to some demand or other they had just made. Anytime this happened, they descended on me, and the handsome one would beg them to stop.

Perhaps, he was performing a kindness.

The handsome one said, *You see what you've caused? Your father was crying like a baby.* At that moment, I hated myself for being careless, for having not confirmed things with my friends in Kano. I had just wanted to try things on my own, for once.

The boy, who I later recognised to be the one who I had been

23 First published in *Translation Magazine*, 2017.

in correspondence with, took my bags and started emptying their contents on the floor. He took my notebooks containing my short stories, my unfinished novel, poems, the few books I had taken with me to the residency. I knew he was looking for anything he could use to identify me. As if we hadn't been talking to each other for more than a fortnight.

* * *

I: Reclamation

I knew this same body would seek solace.
My wrist would heal and forget the knot
that had made my fingers numb, my toes
set in a tremor that made each of them,
my captors, laugh uncontrollably.
I knew my chest would settle one day –
This body would know it was natural
not to fret at the slightest sound of a man
walking in, a phone ringing, a cup falling.

I would begin to recognise this body
as it went from one bedroom to another
as it prepared itself to rest, a ritual
only recently reclaimed, to be grateful

that this persistent pounding in my head
I could, at last, I could hear myself, even now as I lay
on this carpeted floor to write this poem.

II: Consolation

We rehearsed what I would say in this small
cubic room strewn with clothes.

My counsellor told me to prepare
for an event where the footage
would be leaked. I nodded, though I knew
he couldn't see me. My throat hurt;
a day ago, with the kidnappers,
I had cried till I had a sore throat because
my nostrils were plugged with phlegm.
In these brief moments, everything gathered
its own speed: one second I was safe,
waiting in the street on that raining day,
and the next, someone was ramming
a stick into my knees to bring me down,
as if, had he simply asked, I would not
have understood, as if had he not
slapped me, I would not have complied.
I told myself: *this is how you die. Shameless.*
But then it came like a consolation.

III: Stampede

It was only a matter of time,
the shadows would soon start lengthening,
streets brimming with taillights, then I'd see

the ghosts of the young boys who held me,
in the people hurrying, in the man
who bumped into me, saying: *Watch out.*
It would seem that everyone was saying goodbye.
The waning sunsets of May that encroached
into June kept the rain away, so that
I, made a foreigner in my place of birth,
would experience every dark cloud
as impending rain, every man hurrying
in my direction as a stampeding crowd.

IV: In the cyber café

On the day I was held: dusk came, I was freed.
They led me to a tricycle that would wheel me
to the park where I would enter a car
that would lead me to the public bus
that would take me home. I thought I had myself.
Anybody could see that I was crying,
but no one in the car dared to ask me.

I hadn't realised I was shivering
in the cyber café until the man
seated beside me turned to look at my hands
and said, *sorry*, and I nodded slowly.
Some of us will need other people
to tell us that we are shivering,
to remind us to reclaim our bodies.
Some of us will never reclaim our bodies,
some will find, some will be found.
We will have to remain silent to hear
ourselves walking, talking, then sulking.
Some will remain in their houses,
others will be lost to the outside.

Taking a walk in Princess's shoes as she prepares for the Pretoria Parade

CARL COLLISON

PHOTO ESSAY

ABOVE: Heels and healing: Originally from Limpopo, Princess moved to Pretoria in 2011 to study clothing production. She now works as a peer educator for the Wits Reproductive Health and HIV Institute.

OPPOSITE TOP: Facing up: Her daily makeup routine takes her 'at least 35 to 40 minutes' to complete. 'But today I'll do it in 15 minutes, because we have to rush,' she laughs.

OPPOSITE BOTTOM: Brave beauty: The only picture in Princess's bedroom is one she took of herself. 'I love pictures of myself,' Princess smiles. 'I was in Cape Town last week for the opening of Zanele Muholi's exhibition, *Brave Beauties*. She photographed me as part of that show. There were two big pictures of me. It was awesome seeing myself on those gallery walls. Awesome.'

We are family: In the taxi to Pretoria Pride, Princess and another peer educator, Kinnah van Staden, share a laugh. 'We have a really strong bond,' she says of her relationship with her colleagues. 'We are sisters now. We call each other family.'

Health on the go: Princess and the rest of the Wits Reproductive Health and HIV Institute team decorate the mobile clinic.

Contentment: 'Doing this is something I really enjoy. I just love helping people. It's something productive that you're doing,' Princess says.

Queer quorum: For Princess, Pride 'brings people together. People of different cultures … We're all just here to celebrate the queer community,' she says.

Uncovering awareness: Princess and one of her teammates go about preparing the gazebo, from which they do their awareness-raising on the services the institute offers.

A tall, lithe transgender woman with delicate features, Princess may not fit the archetypal image of a nurse. But as a peer educator, she is, to some extent, a health practitioner.

Human settlements

TSHEPISO MABULA
KA NDONGENI

PHOTO ESSAY

172

Drowning

THANDOKUHLE MNGQIBISA

PHOTO ESSAY

'Your kink is not my kink'

African queer women and gender non-conforming persons find sexual freedom in bondage

SIPHUMEZE KHUNDAYI & TIFFANY MUGO

PHOTO ESSAY

Biographies

ISAAC OTIDI AMUKE

Isaac Otidi Amuke lives and writes in Nairobi, Kenya. His reportage/non-fiction has appeared in *Kwani?*, the Commonwealth Writers blog, *Wasafiri*, the World Policy Institute, *Adda Stories*, the *New African Magazine* and the *Chimurenga Chronic*. He contributed the title piece for *Safe House: Explorations in Creative Nonfiction* (Dundurn/Cassava Republic 2016), an anthology of non-fiction from Africa edited by Ellah Wakatama Allfrey. He received the 2013 Jean Jacques Rousseau Fellowship from the Akademie Schloss Solitude in Stuttgart, Germany, and was a finalist for the 2016 CNN Multichoice African Journalist of the Year Awards, where he received the Highly Commended Features Award.

JACO BARNARD-NAUDE

Jaco Barnard-Naude is a professor in Private Law at the University of Cape Town Law Faculty. He is also a published poet and literary critic.

JAYNE BAULING

Jayne Bauling's YA novels have won a number of literary awards, and two of them have been approved as high school set works by the DBE. *Dreaming of Light* was also chosen for the 2014 IBBY Honour List. Her short stories for adults and youth have been published in various anthologies, and have twice been shortlisted for the Commonwealth Short Story Prize. A former Johannesburger, she now lives in White River in Mpumalanga Province.
Twitter: @JayneBauling
Facebook: Jayne Bauling Writer
https://www.facebook.com/Jayne-Bauling-Writer-165514616870712/

EFEMIA CHELA

Efemia Chela was born in 1991 and is a Zambian-Ghanaian writer, literary critic and editor. Her first published story, 'Chicken' was nominated for The 2014 Caine Prize for African Writing. Efemia's subsequent short stories and poems have been published in places like *TOKEN*, *Short.Sharp. Stories: Adults Only*, *New Internationalist*, *Wasafiri* and *PEN Passages: Africa*. Efemia co-edited the 2016 Short Story Day Africa collection, *Migrations*. She is currently the Francophone and Contributing Editor for *The Johannesburg Review of Books* and the Mellon Writer-In-Residence at Rhodes University.

CARL COLLISON

Carl Collison is the Other Foundation's Rainbow Fellow at the *Mail & Guardian*. He has contributed to a range of local and international publications, covering social justice issues as well as art and is committed to defending and advancing the human rights of the LGBTI community in Southern Africa.

PWAANGULONGII DAUOD

Pwaangulongii Dauod is the former creative director at Ilmihouse – an art house in Kaduna, Nigeria – and is a 2016 MacDowell Colony fellow. He is currently working on two books – a collection of essays titled *Africa's Future Has No Space for Stupid Black Men*, and a novel.

PIERRE DE VOS

Pierre de Vos is the Claude Leon Foundation Chair in Constitutional Governance at the University of Cape Town Law Faculty. He writes a popular blog, Constitutionally Speaking, and comments in the media on constitutional and social issues.

CHIKÉ FRANKIE EDOZIEN

Growing up in Lagos, Nigeria, Chiké Frankie Edozien learnt to read from the newspapers his father brought home daily. He grew up to become an ink-stain scribbler telling the stories of others in service of a greater good. He is a contributor to the 2016 Commonwealth Writers anthology, *Safe House: Explorations in Creative Nonfiction* and in 2017 his 'Last night in Asaba' was published by Jalada Africa/Transitions. He is the author of *Lives of Great Men: Living & Loving as an African Gay Man* (Team Angelica).

KIPROP KIMUTAI

Kiprop Kimutai is a Kenyan writer whose fiction has been published by Kwani? Trust, Jalada, *Painted Bride Quarterly*, *No Tokens*, Acre Books, Caine Prize and Farafina. He has participated in premier writing workshops such as the Caine Prize Workshop in 2015 and the Farafina Workshop in 2013. In 2017, he was invited as a panellist for the Franschhoek Literary Festival and the FNS Book Fair in South Africa, and was also shortlisted for the Miles Morland Scholarship. He served as an editor for the anthology *Walking the Tightrope: Poetry and Prose by LGBTQ Writers from Africa*, which archived the lived realities, challenges, dreams, personhood and experiences of queer Africans through poetic verse. The anthology was published by Lethe Press in 2016. He is currently working on his first novel, *The Bantam Chicken Project*.

WELCOME LISHIVHA

Welcome Lishivha is currently a travel journalist for *Getaway* magazine. He completed his undergraduate studies at the University of the Witwatersrand and then went on to complete his Masters in Journalism and Media Studies at Rhodes University. Having recently learnt to ride a bike and swim, you could say he is on a quest to reclaim the childhood he spent mostly indoors watching Oprah. His interests include queer theory, cooking, literature and getting to know people.

SARAH LUBALA

Sarah Lubala is a Congolese-born South African writer. She loves tea, napping and Pablo Neruda's love sonnets (in that order). Her poetry has appeared in *Prufrock*, *Brittle Paper*, *The Missing Slate* and is forthcoming in *Apogee* (Perigree).

TSHEPISO MABULA KA NDONGENI

Tshepiso Mabula is a young photographer and writer born in the Lephalale district of Limpopo, South Africa. Mabula's interest in photography sparked when, during a visit to a family member in 2012, she found award-winning South African photographer Santu Mofokeng's Bloemhof photo book. Mabula explores the small things through photography: exposing the humanity in oppositional, chaotic or even boring environments. She captures the dignity in ordinary people, far removed from the glamorous or ideal atmospheres of high-profile photography. Tshepiso is a storyteller who believes that her calling is to produce work that promotes equity and social unity and seeks to correct the injustices that exist in our everyday culture. To her social justice means being able to embrace our similarities as a people while working towards creating a society where all can live freely without prejudice. Tshepiso is a visual observer of bantu living, a member of the movement against neo-liberal stokvel politics, a non-conformist and a township native working towards owning her first full set of Tupperware dishes.

DAVID MEDALIE

David Medalie is an award-winning short story writer, novelist and anthologist. He has published two collections of short stories, a novel and has edited two anthologies of South African short stories. He teaches literature and creative writing in the Department of English at the University of Pretoria. He lives in Johannesburg.

THANDOKUHLE MNGQIBISA

Thandokuhle Mngqibisa is a medical doctor, internationally published poet and a facilitator with a focus on issues surrounding womxn. She is a teacher for the Mzansi Poetry Academy – the first of its kind in South Africa – and an activist for gender equality. In 2016 she published a chapbook called *Four Stitches*. She is looking to publish a full collection of poetry in 2017/2018. The photograph of Thandokuhle that appears in this anthology was taken in collaboration with Sibongiseni Mngqibisa.

SIPHUMEZE KHUNDAYI & TIFFANY MUGO

Siphumeze Khundayi (SA) and Tiffany Mugo (Kenya) run HOLAAfrica! a queer African womanist digital platform dealing with matters of sex and sexuality as they pertain to African woman. The work of HOLAAfrica! focuses on archiving stories, knowledge production, digital community building and creating spaces that deal with safe sex and pleasure. Tiffany, the curator, is a media consultant and opinions writer pontificating on all things politics and sex. Siphumeze, the artistic director, is a theatre maker, photographer and facilitator whose work revolves around gender and sexual identity.

NICK HADIKWA MWALUKO

Trans, queer, non-binary, genderqueer, genderfuck, gender non-conforming, poet-playwright-fiction-essayist Nick Mwaluko: Plays include: *37, S.T.A.R: Marsha P. Johnson*; 2 queer African trilogies *Waafrika* and *Waafrika 123*; QTPOC trans masculine *S/He: THEY/THEM*; queer apocalypse *Homeless in the AfterLife*; *Blueprint for an African Lesbian*; *S/Heroe*; *Mama Afrika*; *Queering Macbeth*; *To Dyke Trans*; *Gayze* and more. Nick is a two-time recipient of the Creativity Fund from the Public Theater and Time Warner; a 2017 Spring grantee of a TBA Individual Artist Cash grant. Nick graduated Magna Cum Laude from Columbia University, MFA also at Columbia University as a Point Scholar, the largest LGBTQIA scholarship fund, and Columbia University Fellowship.

CHIBỤÌHÈ OBI

Chibụìhè Obi's writings have been published or are forthcoming in *Brittle Paper*, *Expound Magazine*, *Praxis*, *Kalahari Review*, *14: An Anthology of Queer Art*, *Mounting the Moon*, among others. He is the winner of the Brittle Paper Anniversary Award, the Babishai Niwe Haiku Prize and was a 2016 Pushcart Prize nominee.

HAPUYA ONONIME

Hapuya Ononime is a Nigerian writer whose works have appeared in *Threepenny Review*, *Commonwealth Writers*, *The Cincinnati Review*, *Salamander* magazine, *Transition* magazine, *Ambit* magazine, and in *Ruminate* magazine.